T0194160

Dr. Southard has a compassion to serve Christian young people in seeking to be able to integrate the truth of their faith with the life and work that is before them. He speaks from experience. He is a student of the Bible and a committed follower of Jesus Christ. He has founded and developed a successful pharmaceutical company. He understands the challenges of integrating the truths of our Christian faith with the discoveries and theories of science and addresses issues such as evolution, creation, and the age of man.

This book is not only for Christian young people but after reading it I also encourage their parents to read it as well. In doing so, they will be able to give more thoughtful counsel to their children to understand how a family can relate their faith to a rapidly changing world.

C. William Pollard, Former CEO of The ServiceMaster Company and author of the *Tides of Life* and the best seller *The Soul of the Firm*. Currently Chairman of Fairwyn Investment Company.

I am honored to know Dr. Lee Southard, and not only serve as his pastor, but to call him friend. Over the years of our long friendship I have heard Lee's passion to invest in the next generation. Lee is a champion of truth, understanding the power of truth to bring transformation and life. **To Know With Certainty** captures that passion with precision and clarity. It is a powerful tool to prepare young men and women for the most important life-issues they will face.

Dr. Daryl G. Donovan, Senior Pastor, Sanibel Community Church

The genius of this book is that in distinct yet straightforward and understandable terms it clearly identifies those truths that both parents and teenage youth need to know for certain about the Christian faith before college and career. It is a must read that will keep young people from rejecting their faith when challenged by the secular culture prevalent in America and the world today.

John C. (Jack) Dannemiller
former Chairman and CEO of a Fortune 1000 company
and co-founder, Chairman and CEO of Living Dialog Ministries.

Having completed Dr. Lee Southard's "To Know with Certainty" course, I find the knowledge contained within the course and this material to be vital in the reasoning and evidence for my faith. Lee provides compelling topics that show how history and science affirm God's existence, contrary to what society would have students like me believe. The material presented is truly the product of intense research and wisdom, and will help prepare many to defend their faith indefinitely; without fault.

Jacob Goodman,
Student, University of Central Florida

As a youth pastor who has worked with middle school and high school students for over 17 years, I have seen the importance of making sure teens have a sure foundation of what they believe in before they reach college or the working world. I have also worked with several youth leaders throughout my years of ministry, and I have found that working with Lee has been invaluable as he just turned 80 and yet still has a passion to work with teens, something he's been doing for several decades. Whether you are a teen, a parent, a youth leader, or a youth pastor I know you will find Lee's book easy to read and very insightful as it highlights key topics to know and teach as you prepare yourself or others for life "in the real world."

Kevin Shafer,
Youth Pastor, Sanibel Community Church

Dr. Lee Southard has assembled a great tool to combat attacks on high school and college students' faith. After taking the course, I found it easier to uphold my beliefs within the classroom and was less afraid to speak about the science of what I believe.

Matthew Lucker,
Student Swarthmore College

Lee Southard is a man in love with his Creator and passionate about sharing the reasons for that love with today's youth. Lee has taught our son and his fellow students with a listening ear; this book is written with an understanding of the world they live in. As we read the book we were amazed at how Lee was able to include all of the evidence that supports our faith while presenting it in a way that captures both the heart and the intellect of parents and our youth. It is a page-turner because of the passionate heart for Jesus that motivated every chapter.

Ruth Ann and Michael Skaggs,
Parents of a College Student

To Know with Certainty

Answers to Christian Students' Questions Upon Leaving High School

G. LEE SOUTHARD, PH.D.

"Now they know that everything you have given me comes from you. For I gave them the words you gave me and they accepted them. **They knew with certainty** that I came from you, and they believed that you sent me." John 17:7-8

WESTBOW
PRESS®
A DIVISION OF THOMAS NELSON
& ZONDERVAN

WestBow Press books may be ordered through booksellers or by contacting:

WestBow Press
A Division of Thomas Nelson & Zondervan
1663 Liberty Drive
Bloomington, IN 47403
www.westbowpress.com
1 (866) 928-1240

All Scripture quotations in this publication are from the HOLY BIBLE, NEW INTERNATIONAL VERSION ® NIV ® Copyright © 1973, 1978, 1984, 2011 by Biblica, Inc.®. Used by permission. All rights reserved worldwide.

ISBN: 978-1-5127-8633-0 (sc)
ISBN: 978-1-5127-8634-7 (hc)
ISBN: 978-1-5127-8632-3 (e)

Library of Congress Control Number: 2017906756

Print information available on the last page.

WestBow Press rev. date: 5/23/2018

Dedication

To my late wife of 51 years, Marilyn, our four boys Jeff,
Tom, Todd and Brian and my six grandchildren Matt,
Allie, Gabbie, Sabrina, Chase and Christian.

Acknowledgments

In spite of the appealing word's of Frank Sinatra's *I Did it My Way* no one does anything their way solely. Such is the case with this book. Allen Hye, PhD and Roberta Hye, PhD edited the manuscript. In addition my Wednesday morning men's discussion group was helpful as a sounding board for several of the chapters. Among these Jack Dannenmiller was helpful in the publishing strategy and a great encourager. Pierre Loizeaux was helpful in providing biblical insights and Richard Kolvak in evaluating the science. My pastor Dr. Daryl Donovan reminded me that Moses was 80 years old when he went to Egypt to rescue his people. I also acknowledge the support of my wife Nancy during a busy time in our life where she enabled me to find the time to work on the manuscript.

FOREWORD

Dr. Southard, the author of "To Know with Certainty," is a person I have known for many years. Our friendship began in our pre-teen years as neighbors in Richmond, VA. We were both graduates of the Class of 1959 at The Virginia Military Institute, but went in different directions following our graduation; however, we never lost touch with one another.

Dr. Southard was an outstanding Student-Athlete and Leader at The Virginia Military Institute. After his graduation he served his country in the United States Army, and then obtained his MS at George Washington University and his PhD at the University of North Carolina. He is the proud father of four sons, and suffered the loss of his wife Marilyn after 51 years of marriage. As time passed he met Nancy and they were married.

Dr. Southard has worn many hats in his lifetime: husband, father, teacher, Christian, scientist, businessman and many other adventures. In any endeavor he undertook, he put his complete self into it. Dr. Southard is one of those rare individuals who could talk the talk, but more importantly, walk the walk!

He has now added another title to his resume—Author! In his book, "To Know with Certainty," Dr. Southard presents a Christian viewpoint that there is a God, and that God is our Creator of our universe, but as a scientist he does show the role of science in the Creation of the world. He has undertaken this task with his usual dedication, research and thoroughness. He references many verses from the Bible that reinforce his theory that God created the universe, but that science did play a role. These references show Dr. Southard's unique experiences as it related to his being both a

Christian and a scientist. To some "To Know with Certainty" could even be considered as a refresher course of the Bible –it is that precise.

"To Know with Certainty" is directed primarily to the young high school graduate preparing to go to college. In many cases they lose their connection to being a Christian, and perhaps even drop their faith. In my humble opinion, this book should be read by all students, Christian or otherwise. To quote Dr. Southard from "To Know with Certainty," "You do not need to be a soldier or first responder to have your life under attack. The survival of young people facing a world hostile to their faith is no different and it is going on around us right now. It is guaranteed to continue and your child's life depends on a strong faith that cannot be shaken. This is critical—eternity is at stake."

In closing, I would highly recommend Dr. Southard's "To Know with Certainty" as required reading for the approaching college student, but will go a step further, and recommend the same for their parents or guardians.

Robert J. (Bobby) Ross

Bobby Ross was a successful head football coach. His Maryland teams won 4 ACC Championships. He guided his 1990 Georgia Tech squad to the UPI national championship and coached the 1994 San Diego Chargers to an appearance in Super Bowl XXIX. His awards include <u>Bobby Dodd Coach of the Year Award</u>(1990); <u>Paul "Bear" Bryant Award</u> (1990):; <u>Sporting News College Football COY</u> (1990);<u>Walter Camp Coach of the Year</u> (1990); <u>Eddie Robinson Coach of the Year</u> (1990); <u>AFCA Coach of the Year</u> (1991);<u>San Diego Chargers Hall of Fame</u>; <u>San Diego Chargers 50th Anniversary Team</u>

Robert Joseph Ross served as the head football coach at The Citadel (1973–1977), the University of Maryland, College Park (1982–1986), the Georgia Institute of Technology (1987–1991), and the United States Military Academy (2004–2006), compiling a career college football record of 103–101–2. Ross was also the head coach of the National Football League's San Diego Chargers from 1992 to 1996 and the Detroit Lions from 1997 to 2000, tallying a career NFL mark of 77–68. His Maryland teams won 4 ACC Championships (1983-5 and 1990). He guided his 1990

Georgia Tech squad to the UPI national championship and coached the 1994 San Diego Chargers to an appearance in Super Bowl XXIX. His awards include <u>Bobby Dodd Coach of the Year Award(1990)</u>; <u>Paul "Bear" Bryant Award</u> (1990):; <u>Sporting News College Football COY</u> (1990);<u>Walter Camp Coach of the Year</u> (1990); <u>Eddie Robinson Coach of the Year</u> (1990); <u>AFCA Coach of the Year</u> (1991);<u>San Diego Chargers Hall of Fame</u>; <u>San Diego Chargers 50th Anniversary Team</u>

CONTENTS

Preface – A Letter to Parents xix
Introduction – A Letter to Students xxxi

Part I – Apologetics and Church History

Chapter 1 – Some Basic Questions 1
    Does God Exist? 1
    How Does God Speak to Us? 3
    Did Jesus Really Live? If So, Who Was He? 7
    Was Jesus The Messiah and Divine? 9
    What Did Jesus Do to Demonstrate His Divinity? 10
    What Did Jesus Say About Himself? 12
    What Did Others Say About Jesus? 14
    Did Jesus Fulfill Prophecy? 14
    Did Jesus Really Rise From the Dead? 15

Chapter 2 – Is the New Testament True? 21
    Can the Gospels be Trusted? 21
    Did the New Testament Writers Engage in Fabrication? 24
    What Was the "Information Gap"? 25
    Are the New Testament Documents Authentic? 30
    How Close Are the Manuscripts To the Actual Events? 31
    How Sure Are We About The Authors Of The New Testament? . .32
    What about Additions to Scripture? 35
    Why Are There Sometimes Different Descriptions of the Same
        Event? 35
    How Accurately Were New Testament Manuscripts Copied? 36

Chapter 3 – How Did the Christian Church Develop? 39

What Were Some Major Pre-New Testament Events? 40

What Was the Diaspora? 40

What Was the Septuagint? 41

How Did Roman Culture and Infrastructure Help the
Church? 42

What Was the Common Language? 42

What Were Some Major First-Century Events? 43

What Was the Birth of the Christian Church? 43

What Was the Didache? 45

Who Were the Apostolic Fathers? 45

What Were Some Major Second to Fourth-Century Events? 47

What Was the Core Theology of the Early Church? 48

What Were Major Fifth-Century to Seventeenth-Century Events? . .50

Chapter 4 – What Is Your Spiritual DNA? 55

Did Christianity Help Create Western Civilization? 55

Is America a Christian Nation? 58

What Did the Founders Say About Christianity? 62

What About the "Unchristian" Side of American History? 64

Part II – The Convergence of Biblical and Scientific Truth

Chapter 5 – What Is Science? 69

What Is the Definition of Science? 70

What Is Intelligent Design? 70

What Is the Supernatural? 72

What Is Scientific Naturalism? 73

Is There a Conflict Between Science and the Bible? 74

Who Were the Great Scientists? 76

Chapter 6 – What Is Evolution? 81

What Are The Categories of Evolution? 83

What Are Some Things That Question Evolution? 85

What Is Convergent Evolution? 85

What Was the Cambrian Explosion? 86

What Are Transitional Life Forms?........................87

Does Probability Apply To Evolution?.....................88

What Is the DNA Enigma?.............................89

What Is Irreducible Complexity? 90

What Is the Evolutionary Worldview?....................91

Chapter 7 – What About Creation? 95

Was the Creation Planned by God?.......................95

What Was Pre-Creation? 95

What Are the Ten Most Important Words Ever Written?.......98

What About Time? 99

What Was the Big Bang?.............................. 100

What Is Cosmic Time? 102

What Is Geological Time?............................. 102

Was Our Planet Specially Prepared for Humans? 105

Chapter 8 – What About the Origin of Man?.....................107

1. What Is the Young-Earth Model of Man's Origin in Genesis? ..108

2. What is the Old-Earth Model of Man's Origin in Genesis? ... 109

3. What is the Evolution Model? 110

4. What Is the Theistic Evolution Model? 112

Conclusion...115

Appendix..117

A. Prophecies About Jesus.............................117

B. Recommended Resources 121

References 125

A Letter to Parents

"My people are destroyed from lack of knowledge.
Because you have rejected knowledge, I also reject you as
my priests; because you have ignored the law of your God,
I also will ignore your children." Hosea 4:6

Dear Parents,

The prophet Hosea could have had today's world in mind when he
recorded God's words in the above statement: "My people are destroyed from
lack of knowledge." *To Know With Certainty* came into being because of my
concern about the growing number of young people who, on graduating from
high school without a sufficient knowledge and intellectual understanding of
their beliefs, lose touch with the church and drop out of the faith.

While this book is primarily a tool to help train and equip your children
in their Christian faith, I trust that it will also be a resource for you in
shaping and encouraging them as children of God. You as parents play the
most important role in helping your children develop and guard their faith.
You will do this by modeling a Christian lifestyle and through instruction.

There is an urgent need for children and parents to understand the
importance of knowing with certainty where they stand with God, so that
they may live the life God ordained for them. They must also be able to
understand, defend, and contend for the Christian faith on an intellectual
basis. These are the reasons why this book was written.

My wife and I raised four boys during from the 1960s to the mid-1990s.
During those years we believed that many traditional values that had their
origins in the Christian faith were being compromised —values that had

made this country great and allowed its citizens to live full lives. As a result, we made every effort to prepare our boys for the challenges of life in an often hostile society. We found that task stressful then, but the culture in which we raised our boys seemed simpler and far less threatening than the one you face in raising your children today. *To Know With Certainty* was written with you and your child in mind, but they are not the only ones who need the information in this book. You do too, because you are the key to reshaping what is happening in society today, and it starts in the home. I hope in this letter to convince you of that.

For generations now, young people transitioning out of high school into college or careers have been doing so with ever less commitment to the values of the Christian faith; indeed, they have been leaving the church. Numerous surveys substantiate this, and no one is immune as the exodus from Christianity cuts across social and economic levels, including mainline and evangelical Protestant denominations and Catholics as well. If this trend is not halted, there will be profound consequences for the church and the nation. The second President of the United States, John Adams, recognized this when he said," America's success depends on the Christian faith."

Why Are Young People Leaving the Faith?

Surveys indicate that if teens are not **trained** in the Christian faith by the time they graduate from high school, there is a high likelihood that they will succumb to secular, godless pressures, with dire results. David Kinnaman and Aly Hawkins have noted that American teenagers are religiously active, but the twenty-somethings are among the least religiously active (22). As many as 70% of *Christian* young adults ages 18-29 will drop out or step away from their faith for at least one year, and 46% of these will never return to the church. **This means that about one-third of all Christian young adults in this age group are forever lost to the church and perhaps their Christian faith** (Barna, "Six Reasons").

How Can We Keep Them In the Faith?

After such dismal statistics this is a reasonable question. In a word it is **training**, knowing what to do when it is needed. When life is threatened, staying alive can depend on training. Ask any soldier or first responder who has been in tense and life-threatening situations, "How did you survive?" They will always reply, "My training kicked in." They were ready and instinctively responded to the challenge when the training was needed. You do not need to be a soldier or first responder to have your life under attack. The survival of young people facing a world hostile to their faith is no different, and it is going on all around us right now. It is guaranteed to continue and your child's life depends on a strong faith that cannot be shaken. This is critical—eternity is at stake.

As with the soldier, one's spiritual instincts should kick in when faith is challenged. This requires training, as you parents have recognized in raising your child with the help of the church. There is an optimum window of opportunity to train and equip your kids' in their faith: this window is just before high school graduation, during the junior and senior years, and in the summer before they leave for college or careers. It is a time when teens are intellectually maturing and inquisitive about their lives and future. Students are ready to learn, because they know they will be entering a new and exciting phase of life. They *and you* should be concerned about anything that would derail their progress toward a richer life in Christ.

The Faith Is Not Being Passed On

Another reason teens leave the church is that **"Older generations of Americans are not passing along the Christian faith as effectively as their forebears"** (emphasis added; Pew, 5-12-2015). A main reason for this is family mobility, where many families live distant from grandparents, uncles, and aunts. Parents, grandparents, uncles, and aunts are all in the training business. *"Start children off on the way they should go, and even when they are old they will not turn from it"* (Proverbs 22:6).

Influence of Changing Culture

Christianity was once very important to America's culture. In recent years Christianity has been progressively minimized in America's culture to the point where it is becoming viewed more as irrelevant. There are a variety of explanations for this changing culture; a complete discussion can be found in David Kinnaman and Gabe Lyons' book *Good Faith*.

Cultural pressures cause Christians to "back off" from being confident and expressive about their faith. Society says, "It is not politically correct," and we have bought into it. That should be the last consideration for Christians, because we are beholden to a higher authority who has given us a written guarantee of what we must do to have eternal life. We have a divine commander-in-chief who has issued clear orders to be declarers of the faith (Mathew 28:19-20). These orders have been proven correct—events have shown that the way of the world is not the answer to life's questions. Rather, the answer is keeping your child Christian. This has proven to be the right choice if you want the best for your child.

Every parent should consider the results of The National Study on Youth and Religion, a 15-year study ending in 2015 that documented the religious lives of American youth as they move into adulthood. For 12th- graders, **risk behaviors any parent would be concerned about are less likely to occur if the child is participating in religious activities. The results are not even close.** These risk behaviors are: substance abuse, including smoking and drinking, being involved in crime and violence, having school problems, and engaging in unsafe or unconstructive activities. Factors shown by the survey to be important in minimizing risk behaviors and their consequences were: **frequency of church attendance, the importance of religion to the child, years of youth group involvement, and denomination** (Smith and Faris). Note how many of these factors are driven in the family by parents and the same factors influence positively the success of the child.

It was found that religious 12th-graders have significantly higher self-esteem and hold more positive attitudes about life in general than their less religious peers. The encouraging indicators are these: teens hold positive attitudes toward themselves, enjoy life as much as anyone, feel like their lives are useful, feel hopeful about their futures, feel satisfied with their lives, feel like they have something of which to be proud, feel good to be alive, feel that life is meaningful, and enjoy being in school.

Several years ago when I first read these studies, I thought to myself, **"This is an 'aha!' moment. Knowing these results, why would any parent not do the necessary things noted above to have their children achieve these results?"** One almost wants to scream this out loud to American parents. So let me ask you parent,"Why would you not want to be in church and have your child in church getting trained and equipped?"

Influence of Secondary Education

For a very long time this country's educational system has been under the influence of secular humanism. As a result, the system has contributed significantly to young people leaving the Christian faith and the church. There is good reason why this is true.

C.F. Potter, the author of *Humanism: A New Religion* (1930), wrote, **"Education is thus a most powerful ally of humanism and every American public school is a school of humanism. What can the theistic Sunday schools, meeting for an hour once a week and teaching only a fraction of the children, do to stem the tide of a five-day program of humanistic teaching?"** (128). The point Potter makes is this: the intellectual influence in school that excludes God has about 40x more time to sink into a student's mind than whatever intellectual countermeasures the student is able to get in church, and more than what the child gets at home.

Potter is right. The church has the youth for one day a week, for one hour of Sunday school (hopefully) and maybe one hour of worship, if they attend at all. If the kids are in a youth group, there may be another one to three hours of Christian educational time during the week.

Recognizing the success of humanist-based education, leading secular humanist Paul Blanshard pronounced, **"I think the most important factor leading us to a secular society has been the educational factor. Our schools may not teach Johnny to read properly, but the fact that Johnny is in school until he is sixteen tends to lead toward the elimination of religious superstition. The average child now acquires a high school education, and this militates against Adam and Eve and all other myths of alleged history"** (25). Johnny is receiving a humanist-driven intellectual understanding about his world to the exclusion of God's role in it.

The Influence of Atheism in Colleges and Universities

As Christians we believe in God and recognize a basic truth that God was, in the words of the hymn, *My Country, "Tis of Thee*, the "Author of liberty" and our beliefs. Both atheism and agnosticism are also beliefs, because the former believes there is no God and the latter believes one does not know whether there is a God. Atheism and agnosticism, while growing, still represent a small part of the American populace, but because they are in significant positions of influence in education, their power to wield that influence is enhanced.

According to the Pew Research Center in 2014, atheists comprised 3.1% and agnostics 4.0% of the total U.S. population. From such a small minority of the population, one might expect little influence on our young people. However, it is not the number but the strategic position of atheists, particularly in academia, that gives their views toward God such influence. The chance of your children being in a classroom where their faith might be influenced by someone not believing in God is considerable.

Disbelief in God by academics in the basic scientific disciplines reportedly is as follows: Physics 40.8%, Chemistry 26.6%, and Biology 41.0%. There is disbelief in other college disciplines: Sociology 34.0%, Economics 31.7%, Political Science 27.0%, and Psychology 33% (Ecklund and Scheitle). Another study found that in America's colleges and universities nearly 64% of biologists and social scientists identified themselves as atheists or agnostics (Ecklund, 2/7/2007, 2). And for scientists who are leaders in the field of evolution, 87% deny the existence of God, 88% do not believe in life after death, and 90% reject the idea that there is a an ultimate purpose to evolution (Graffin and Provine).

This is not to say that every professor will be out to destroy your children's faith, but these results would suggest that the chances of their sitting in a classroom of a professor with a worldview different than what you would hope for are significant. This is a question worth investigating when you consider colleges and make your pre-college campus visits.

Perhaps belief in God is only a small part of the answer. The rest of the answer may be in worldviews. Again we go to the work of Gross showing that professors are considerably more left-wing or liberal than the general population of adults. He found that 50% of professors describe themselves as being "left or liberal." About 9% of college faculty members were described as "far left" or "radical." Moderates came out to be 19%, economic conservatives 4%, and social and pro-military conservatives 23%. Thus, academia has developed a self-selection effect in which godless and liberal professors migrate to it and stay there, while conservatives often are dissuaded from joining it.

Study in a field of science poses the highest risk. Fifty-two percent of teens in Christian youth groups say that they intend to pursue a career in a field relating to science and technology (Kinnaman and Hawkins, 140). Given the above statistics about the science faculty in universities and colleges, there should be great concern among parents and teens contemplating a major in these fields. Parents and teens alike should be prepared for decisions that will affect the rest of their lives and their everlasting life.

However, let me also be reassuring regarding a science major. As you will see later in this book, it is science that provides the best tangible evidence for God and His work to make this planet habitable for us. Not all colleges calling themselves Christian are equally faithful to their calling, but if you seek carefully, you can find excellent Christian colleges and professors who will train your children well in the sciences and also build up their faith.

Let me direct you to two excellent web site resources. One is InterVarsity Christian Fellowship, an outstanding campus ministry with chapters at a great many college and universities. Its Emerging Scholars Network with blogs by Christian professors in the field of science is reassuring to Christian students and parents alike. The other is Meet the Prof, affiliated with the prominent campus ministry Cru (formerly Campus Crusade), which has dozens of personal and professional testimonies by Christian professors from many disciplines.

The Church Has Not Done Its Job.

Both the church and parents must recognize that teens need an intellectual understanding of their faith showing that God was and still is a part of the things they learn in the classroom. Surveys asking why teens and young adults leave the church point to a lack of intellectual understanding of their faith, because the reasons they cite for leaving are intellectually based. Thirty-six percent **of post-high-school Christians say they left the church because of:**

- Intellectual skepticism or doubt.
- Faith did not make sense anymore.
- Too many questions they did not think were answered (creation, evolution, sex) by the church.

In a similar analysis, Brian Housman of LifeWay Research, citing several studies, gave the following reasons and explanations for how the church has been failing to train and equip its youth:

1. Shallow belief system.

My book, *To Know With* Certainty, exploring the science and biblically-based facts about God, points teens to God and deepens their belief system.

2. No room for doubt.

The church must recognize that doubt is normal and acceptable, but it also needs to teach the facts that address a student's doubts. This book does that by providing answers to critical questions. It stresses, as the Bible says, "confidence in what we hope for and assurance about what we do not see" (Hebrews 11:1).

3. Exclusive faith.

In a loving manner, this book wants to welcome inquiries and present the case for God and Christ in a factual, scholarly manner. It is not to be exclusive or elitist toward those who may not think as we do. Rather, it wishes to state the facts and let the facts speak for themselves.

4. No answers for opposition.

This book is all about knowing with certainty and creating confidence to not only *defend* but also *contend* for the faith. It is about a Christian using an intellectually-based argument to answer questions about the faith.

Housman went on to reference work at Fuller Theological Seminary that examined why some teenagers had succeeded at having a long-term faith into adulthood. The results were compiled in the book *Sticky Faith: Everyday Ideas to Build Lasting Faith in Your Kids*, by Kara E. Powell and Chap Clark. They found that about 60% of students will walk away from their faith and many of these will not return, but the 40% that did stay had something that made them stay. What was the "something" that produced such grounded children? There was no one thing, but these three factors were vital to the students who stayed with the faith:

1. Being raised in a faith culture that emphasized a relationship with Christ as opposed to adherence to a set of rules.
2. Being surrounded by an intergenerational faith community.
3. **The most important factor by far in each of the lives of teens who developed sticky faith was having parents who were willing to walk with them through their faith journey.** The church could support this by providing (a) training for parents or (b) adult leadership for teens. This book would provide a basis for both.

What Can a Parent Do?

This may not be you, but as noted in a study by the Barna Group, **there is often a great difference between the biblical responsibility that parents feel they have for their children's religious training (Deuteronomy 6:7) and what parents actually do.** The study concluded that 85% of parents of kids under age thirteen believe they have the primary responsibility for teaching their children about religious beliefs and spiritual matters (May 6, 2003). While the study was for parents of children under thirteen, it is unlikely the data would be any different for parents of high school kids. Related research shows that more than 50% of parents do not spend any time on religious or spiritual matters. Thus, churches have an opportunity and obligation to help, by equipping parents to train their children and by supplementing parental training with activities at the church. **If your church cannot help, find another church! But it is really up to you.**

The overall problem has been summed up well by Pastor Jerry Vines: "We are bringing up a generation of young people who are sitting ducks for the secular culture. When they head off to college, they don't receive a solid biblical worldview, and many fall off one by one and reject outright the teachings of the Bible" (Cited by Yarbrough, 31).

Not everyone can attend a Christian college, and even some Christian colleges can be disappointing in addressing the faith/science tension. Nevertheless, there is a good chance your students will end up in higher education and a 100% chance of their encountering a secular environment that challenges their faith. Therefore, both parents and their children would do well to know with certainty the essentials of their faith, so they can, at a minimum, defend it when faced with liberal or godless views and, better yet, engage others with reasonable arguments to lead them to faith. This argues for parents and the church to do a better job of preparing children for life beyond high school. Parents and their children should be learning what is in this book and taking the course based upon it.

What If Nothing Is Done?

As the saying goes, the definition of insanity is continually doing the same thing the same way and getting undesirable results. If families and churches continue to neglect intellectual training, they will continue to see their young people fall away from the faith. According to George Barna, these are the indicators of spiritual decline among evangelical Christian youth:

- 63% of teenaged Christians said they do not believe that Jesus was the Son of God;
- 51% do not believe Jesus rose from the dead;
- 68% do not believe the Holy Spirit is a real entity;
- 33% say that the church will play a part in their lives when they leave home. That means that for 67% the church will not play a role (Barna, 1999).

These figures can only be more alarming now. We can blame the educational system, the church, or the media, but lack of discipline and responsibility in the home is the primary reason for these trends. Anyone working in church youth groups can verify this by observing the behavioral difference between kids whose parents believe in instilling Christian values in their children, and those kids whose parents who are indifferent. This presents an opportunity for the church to reinforce what the believing parents teach and reach out to the children of non-believers. The church must expect certain challenges in reaching out to children who have no parental support for their Christian education, but this is no reason not to try. The same is true for reaching out to parents.

How Can This Book Help?

This book is not about battling statistical trends; statistics only indicate there is a problem. **This book aims to address the problem and sound a call to arms among teens and parents.** The problem is that young people do not know with certainty what they need to know in order to be intellectually equipped for the life they will live. Sadly, most parents do not know either. This book aims to increase your children's understanding and commitment to the faith and make them not only defenders but also bold declarers of the faith. Let's join together and do it!

Failure of the church and you as a parent to collectively embrace the mission of equipping children in the Christian faith to the level it once was will place the church at risk. That in turn will place the United States of America at risk. This is the most important national security issue facing our nation.

Sincerely,

Lee Southard, Ph.D.

INTRODUCTION

A Letter to Students

"For though we live in the world, we do not wage war as the world does. The weapons we fight with are not the weapons of the world. On the contrary, they have divine power to demolish strongholds. **We demolish arguments and every pretension that sets itself against the knowledge of God,** and we take captive every thought to make it obedient to Christ." (2 Corinthians 10:3-5)

Dear Students,

You live in an increasingly complex world full of challenges to your faith. It will require courage to stand firm in the face of these challenges and intellectual prowess when others attack your beliefs, particularly someone in a position of trust or authority, such as a college professor. **The primary purpose of this book is** to strengthen you intellectually to defend and contend for your faith while confidently living as the person God wants you to be.

There is a war going on for the minds of America's children, and that includes yours. This book is in response to that war. It will also serve those parents who are fed up with not being able to respond and to provide their kids with the means to counter intellectually those who ridicule and scorn their faith.

At the root of the inability to engage in a defense of or a contention for one's faith is doubt about the faith. However, if you inquire,,seek the truth and try to know with certainty doubt will give way and produce a strong faith. Noted Christian author Philip Yancey has written on the subject of doubt and what to do about it. Doubt is one of the by-products of the mind God gave humans when he created us, and throughout the Bible there are stories of doubt. Our doubts are usually about the big questions concerning the faith. This book will provide answers to those questions. If you are an honest seeker of truth, there is no excuse for not knowing the evidence for the truth.

Today we have the advantage of looking back over billions of years and, more specifically, at the 2,000 years since the birth of Christ, and we find a vast accumulation of evidence that is more easily accessible than ever. Evidence is defined as the available body of facts or information indicating whether a belief or proposition is true or valid. The fields of theology, science, archeology, and history come together to provide significant and substantial evidence pointing to a purposeful and sovereign God involved in the creation of the universe, the earth and the origin of man. They provide evidence for God's hand in the Christian faith and its role in the development of Western Civilization, including the United States of America.

It is my fervent hope that you not become a statistic, blindsided by the challenges that await you, but a spiritual warrior ready to stand up and give an account of your faith at any time. I wish to equip you to meet confidently and courageously the intellectual and spiritual challenges of modern, secular society, whether at college or in the work world. I want you to "know with certainty" that Jesus is Lord and that He was sent by a sovereign God to bring salvation to a sinful world.

The disciples in John 17 "knew with certainty" because they were eyewitnesses to the life of Jesus and the events of the New Testament. Being an eyewitness to Jesus is no longer possible. Today, certainty must be gained from historical evidence, scientific research and discoveries, and the witness of mature Christian role models guided by a faithful relationship to God through His Holy Spirit. The world wants to treat the Christian message as pure dogma, not grounded in fact, but nothing could be further from the truth. Christianity is a fact-based faith that can be confidently proclaimed and intellectually defended. It is all in the evidence.

Over the three years of Jesus' ministry he consistently taught and equipped twelve men to know with certainty the things of God. How did they do? Jesus announced the results to God: "Now they know that everything you have given me comes from you. For I gave them the words you gave me and they accepted them. They knew with certainty that I came from you, and they believed that you sent me" (John 17:7-8).

The disciples were no longer of the world as Jesus was not of the world. Their knowing with certainty had so strengthened their faith that they were more like Him. Later, when they were empowered by the Holy Spirit, they would take that certainty and teach and preach everywhere in their known world. Through these twelve Jesus built a community of believers, a church that began in the first century and has lasted for 2,000 years. These twelve changed the world. Can you too be so certain, knowing what you stand for and going forth confidently? Yes, you can. When an informed mind and the heart are in sync, you can confidently engage intellectually with anybody you meet. Knowledge without belief is just an academic exercise. Belief with knowledge will strengthen your witness in every situation you encounter. Knowing with certainty means that you are intellectually convinced that what you believe in your heart is true, and you can defend it or contend for it if called upon.

Defense of the faith is called **apologetics**, and this is an apologetics book. It focuses on issues that are often challenged intellectually and that you, therefore, must address intellectually. The word comes from the Greek *apologia*, which means a defense or an account of one's beliefs or position. I have never liked the word because of our common understanding of the English word "apologize," that is, to say "I'm sorry." The word "apologetics" sounds like we Christians have something to apologize for, but we don't. When it comes to faith in God, there is no need to apologize. Instead, the defense of the faith has to be backed up by a ready offense where one knows with certainty what one is talking about. Every football fan has heard the saying, "defense wins championships." An example is the 2016 Super Bowl 50 where the Denver Bronco defense smothered the vaunted offense of the Carolina Panthers. In reality, defense helps to win championships, but you still have to outscore the opponent, and that requires an offense, putting points on the board. You need to understand your faith so that you can both defend and contend for the faith.

An important reason for this book is to promote Christian apologetics. Possessing knowledge of the faith and facing challenges from without make us better apologists. There are multiple examples of effective apologists in the Bible. Consider the Book of Acts, where Peter and later Paul are brought before the Jewish leaders to give an account of why they were preaching a message that the Jews found foreign. Both Peter and Paul recounted the factual history of the Jewish faith and its prophecies and explained in their preaching of the Good News how those prophecies were now coming true. This was the method they employed and the method that you can use. Peter and Paul knew with certainty what they believed.

Another goal of this book is to help train young Christian men and women like you not only to guard the faith but also to declare it with confidence in any setting, articulating what you believe to an unbelieving culture, by going on offense as in the football analogy. *To Know With Certainty* will help you be a Christian witness to many who may not accept the Bible as truth but question it on an intellectual basis. For this you need to be able to contend in a discussion intellectually, meaning you must know the facts. By referencing historical, archaeological, and scientific facts that converge with and reinforce biblical truth, you can reach common ground with such people without compromising your beliefs. You can defend as well as be proactive, confidently mounting a defense of your faith and also going on the offensive in a thoughtful and engaging manner to lead others to a saving faith in Jesus Christ.

Here are ten expectations, which, if met, will enable you to contend confidently for your faith against intellectual challenges in any environment.

1. Know the evidence for the existence of God and state it;
2. Know how God speaks to you and how to speak back;
3. Know the evidence for Jesus as an historical person and state it;
4. Know the evidence for Jesus' death and resurrection and state it;
5. Know the evidence for the authenticity of the Bible and state it;
6. Know the historical evidence for the role that the church played in Western Civilization and state it;
7. Know the evidence for Christian influence in the making of America and state it;
8. Know the strengths and weaknesses of the Theory of Evolution and state them;
9. Know the evidence that supports the Bible and God as creator of the heavens and the earth and state it;
10. Know the evidence that supports God as the creator of man and state it.

To successfully defend and proclaim the Christian faith, you must understand and accept the principle of **God's sovereignty**, His power over all of creation, and live accordingly. This is an essential teaching, because many people today believe that God is not in control and that Satan and man's own free will have taken over from God. Some people think that God is losing, but nothing could be further from the truth. The sovereign God does not release control ever! God's sovereignty extends to everything. This means every action, event, and happening in the past, the present, and in the future is under His control.

God's sovereignty means sovereignty over everyone who ever lived, is living today, or will live in the future, whether a believer in God or not. Only a sovereign God could have had a plan before the creation of the world to make us holy and blameless in His sight. Only a sovereign God could have carried out that plan by exquisitely creating the universe, the earth, and all life as the visible and tangible signs of his greatness. Only a sovereign God could carry out that plan by entering into the world to forgive sin to make men free, and then present a reliable and authentic New Testament to document His plan. Only a sovereign God could have developed the Church, whose actions throughout history would one day lead to the finest nation ever on earth. As you seek to follow God, sovereignty is a key to understanding who He is.

To Know With Certainty is set up in two parts with eight chapters:

Part I - Apologetics and Church History.

Chapter 1 poses some important fundamental questions about Christianity, the answers to which will help enrich your faith and enable you to engage others with confidence as a more effective witness. These questions are at the heart of our faith— "Does God Exist?" "Does He Speak to Us?" and "Did Jesus Really Live?" "Did Jesus Really Rise From the Dead?" Reinforced by a great deal of biblical and scientific fact, we can enthusiastically answer, "Yes!" Right at the beginning we want to establish a biblical and non-biblical basis for God's existence and allow the rest of the book to add to that understanding. By the end of Chapter 1 you should know the wealth of evidence for the existence of God the Father and Jesus.

In **Chapter 2** we explore the question "Is the New Testament True?"

This question is critical if we are to believe in Jesus, because everything we know about him comes from the New Testament. In this chapter you will understand the authenticity, inerrancy, accuracy, reliability, and truth of the Bible as Holy Scripture. There are abundant and excellent resources available to support the truth claims of the New Testament. Like Chapter 1 this chapter is also fundamental to our study, because if you cannot accept the truth of the New Testament, or the entire Bible for that matter, then citing the supporting facts of science is pointless. Understanding the reliability and historical background of the Bible will help you meet intellectual challenges that come your way concerning the truth of your faith.

Chapter 3 investigates the development of the Christian church beginning with Jesus' disciples—they were eyewitnesses to His miracles, teaching, and resurrected body. We learn how the followers of the disciples, known as the Church Fathers, testified to what they heard from eyewitnesses and also carried the story of salvation throughout the known world. The theology surrounding salvation has been passed down unchanged over the intervening 2,000 years. This chapter's brief survey of church history will take you from pre-New Testament events through the Reformation.

In **Chapter 4** we explore the question "Is America a Christian Nation?" by tracing our roots, our spiritual DNA, back to the first century in Jerusalem and along our ancestors' path to America. We learn that, were it not for Christianity, there would have been no Western Civilization, only minimal scientific progress, and no America as we know it. From Pentecost to Jamestown and up until today, the influence of Christianity on society has collectively made us who we are. The Holy Spirit was the catalyst unleashed at Pentecost, and the Christian church was the conduit for these influences on the course of human history leading to America. You will see the contribution of Christianity to the development of reason, the development of science, the birth of freedom, and the moral code. You will also become aware of some controversial chapters in church history and the steps that were taken to right past wrongs.

Part II – The Convergence of Biblical and Scientific Truth

Chapter 5 begins with the premise that the Bible is true, as it claims to be, and that science is a search for truth. Sometimes these two arenas appear to be in conflict, but in fact there is more harmony and convergence when they are examined closely This chapter explores that convergence and introduces some important concepts of science that may not be taught in school because they indicate there might be a creator or designer. It also introduces you to some of history's greatest scientists who were Christians.

Chapter 6 addresses the important and controversial question of evolution. Here, you will become familiar with the different types of evolution, the age of the earth, and the Genesis account of Creation. It will become clear that some types of evolution can be reconciled to the biblical account, while others cannot. In recent times, major aspects of evolution that are still being taught have even fallen out of favor with scientists.

Evolution is a controversial topic because it is generally taught in our schools without acknowledgment of a creator God and without admitting the deficiencies of the theory. In recent years, science and mathematics have indicated the improbability if not impossibility of certain aspects of naturalism and evolution that are routinely taught in our schools. Evolution is void of a creationist view, and it has taken on a worldview proportion that puts it at odds with Christianity.

Chapter 7 is the first of two sections on the sometimes contentious but often complementary relationship between faith and science. It addresses central questions about God's existence and His handiwork in the creation of the universe, such as the Big Bang and our place on a planet that appears to be divinely prepared for human habitation. In this section, we first define the conflict that exists between young-earth and old-earth creationists. Then we study the convergence of truths revealed in the Bible and later confirmed by scientific research.

The ten most important words ever written are "In the beginning God created the heavens and the earth." These words initiate God's plan developed before creation. Everything in life stems from the creation event where the majesty and glory of the sovereign God is demonstrated. Science and the Bible should not be viewed as antagonists. Rather, science helps us to understand our almighty creator whose design is ever present. The truth of the science of the creation can be a powerful witnessing tool for Christian believers.

Chapter 8 is concerned with the origin of man. We will again examine the Bible and science to demonstrate how science supports the biblical narrative on the origin of Adam. We will explore five models of creation, four of which show God in control of the origin of man, the crown of God's creation. You will see how science and the Genesis story can agree without compromising the Bible. When you are armed with this information, your future biology classes should become a place where the wonderment of God's creation comes to life in you.

Following the **Conclusion** you will find an **Appendix** containing a list of prophecies about Jesus and a list of recommended resources for your further study and enjoyment. There is also a list of **References** consulted for or cited in the book. Unless otherwise noted, all biblical quotations are taken from the *New International Version* (NIV).

As I told your parents in my letter to them, it is my hope to help equip you intellectually for your Christian journey. This book encourages you to increase your understanding of and commitment to Christianity and become not only defenders but also bold declarers of the faith. The data is in and it says that you will be a better person all around in this life and ready for the life to come. However, in the final analysis you are responsible for you. It <u>is</u> up to you.

But let me tell you. Your choice to become better equipped in the Christian faith will have two benefits. The first one is eternal in a full life with Christ. That alone should be sufficient.

Secondly, you can help reverse an alarming trend in America where the decreasing influence of the Christian faith may lead to an America whose promises you seek will not be there for you.

Let's just do it!

Sincerely,

Lee Southard, Ph.D.

PART I

Apologetics and Church History

CHAPTER 1

Some Basic Questions

Does God Exist?

Everyone has probably asked the question at some point, "Is there a God?" It is one of the most fundamental questions we humans ask ourselves. The Old Testament uses about sixteen names for God, some more often than others. They all refer to the same God, but usage in the Hebrew language infers a particular meaning often indicating a special characteristic of God. The one used over two thousand times and first used in Genesis 1 is Elohim. It simply means God, and He is the God of the Jews and Christians. There are many gods to many people of the world, but for this study when we say God, we are talking about the God of the Judeo-Christian Bible. He told us in His Word that He exists, and He provided a lot of evidence.

We humans seem to require evidence to believe anything as sure. We ask the question if God exists, and the evidence around us seems as though God is shouting, "Hey, I exist. Just look around you and take it in! I not only exist but have done some wonderful things just for you—so that you can live with me forever."

First, let's look at the evidence that there is no God. Oh, wait, we can't, because *there is no evidence that there is no God. There is only evidence that there is a God*, which we will present in three arguments: cosmological, teleological, and anthropic. Interestingly, it is science that provides tangible evidence that God exists, and that begins at creation.

The Cosmological Argument

The cosmological argument holds that, because the universe came from nothing, it had to have a beginning. For something to have a beginning, there must be a cause or a beginner. A beginner is a creator. Christians and Jews call that creator God. The very first words of the Bible reflect that: "In the beginning God *created* the heavens and the earth." Just as the Bible says and science demonstrates, all matter, space, and time began from nothing. With the big bang, the explosion that put the universe in motion, scientific evidence points back to a moment in time about 13.8 billion years ago when the eternal God created space, time, and matter *ex nihilo*, or out of nothing. The earth was formed around nine billion years ago,[1] all in agreement with Genesis 1:1. Some skeptics say the universe has always existed, but the latest science has proved this to be absolutely wrong. The universe is expanding, and the expansion is accelerating, which means that the universe must have had a beginning.

The Teleological Argument

This argument posits that evidence for a creator or designer is evident everywhere in nature. Science has wonderfully shed a vast amount of light on how the universe and life itself came into being and now operates. It also shows us that certain processes appear to require information to function, indicating some form of intelligence. These processes are so complex that the likelihood of them having come about by chance is exceedingly remote. The term used to describe this is *intelligent design*.

Intelligent design is a scientific theory that employs the methods commonly used by other historical sciences. It concludes that certain features of the universe and of living things are best explained by an intelligent cause, not an undirected process such as natural selection. One aspect of intelligent design is illustrated by organs, processes, or devices that are termed "irreducibly complex" (about which more information can be found in chapter 6), such as the DNA (deoxyribonucleic acid) synthesis

---

[1] This dating of the earth is generally accepted by science. The question of a young-earth versus an old-earth reading of Genesis will be addressed in chapters 7 and 8.

of a protein, the formation and function of the eye, or the cascade of events leading to the clotting of blood. These examples, it is argued, cannot have evolved over time by improving on an existing process. Rather, they can only function as complete entities; the omission of just one part would cause the object not to function as designed.

Many atheists would share this view today, even though they are not ready to concede that the source might be God. In 2007 British philosopher Anthony Flew, an outspoken atheist, wrote a book titled *There Is a God: How the World's Most Notorious Atheist Changed His Mind*. Among the reasons that he gave are the signs pointing to a creative intelligence.

The Anthropic Principle

This argument states that the earth has precisely the right conditions to support human life; any changes to the balance of our planet would prevent the existence of life as we know it. The sun, moon, and planets were placed in just the right position to support life on earth, and the earth's chemistry and physics work together to support life. Significant among the factors that lead to the anthropic principle are the physical constants that govern the universe and our solar system. Each of these constants controls the relationship of precise forces that, were they any less precise, would not support life. The precision to which these constants are fine-tuned is testimony to an intelligence behind our universe; it could not have occurred by chance alone.

How Does God Speak to Us?

In the Old Testament, God first spoke directly to Adam, Noah, and later Moses. Then He spoke to His people through the prophets. In the New Testament, God spoke through Jesus. Hearing from Jesus was like hearing directly from God because Jesus was God. While the audible voice of God may not be heard, there are many ways to hear God. In fact, there are more ways to hear God today than at any other time in history. If you want to hear God, you must be seriously seeking Him. Seeking God means prayer, which is one of the ways to hear God. Seeking God also means using our intellect as we learn more about God's creation and think about the things of God.

The apostle Paul said it best many years ago: "Finally, brothers, whatever

3

is true, whatever is noble, whatever is right, whatever is pure, whatever is admirable—if anything is excellent or praiseworthy—*think* about these things … and the God of peace will be with you" (Philippians 4:8–9) (my emphasis).

In many respects, this book, *To Know with Certainty*, is the result of thinking about "these things" and praying about them. Therefore, it is helpful to understand how God has communicated to His people from the very beginning. When we teach about knowing the truth of His Word, the life of Jesus, creation, the God of history, and His sovereignty, we do so from a basis of what God has revealed to us. This book examines these revelations in order to defend the truth against the rising antagonism of a skeptical culture.

God first communicated to humans orally by speaking a command. He told Adam that he could eat of any tree in the garden, but He commanded Adam not to eat of the tree called the Tree of Knowledge of Good and Evil. As we know, Adam and his wife, Eve, disobeyed God and ate of the tree, and sin entered the world. Ever since this disobedience, sin has been with us and is the root of all of the world's problems. As disappointed as God was in Adam and Eve for disobeying Him, He never stopped communicating with them; He spoke directly with them and with their children. He continued speaking to subsequent generations, often through chosen people we call prophets. These individuals obeyed God to do His will, and to some He spoke prophetically about what He would do in the future. God did not limit Himself to certain people, but He spoke in various ways to every person of every generation, even today.

God Speaks to Us:

Through His Word

About six-thousand-plus years ago, God spoke directly to humans—the pinnacle of His creation. God speaks to us through His spoken and written words that make up the Bible. The Old Testament written accounts are full of God's speaking directly to people like Adam, Noah, Abraham, and Moses. Sometimes He spoke through His chosen prophets like Isaiah, Jeremiah, Ezekiel, and Daniel, including about what He would do in the future. In the New Testament, He speaks to us through the written accounts of Jesus's life in the four gospels and through the epistles, which describe the ministry of the early church that God had planned all along (Ephesians 3:10). We are told by the apostle Paul in 2 Timothy 3:16 that "all scripture is God breathed," meaning that the entire Bible came from God. New Testament scripture contains what God wants us to know about: Jesus's life, His teachings, and His sacrifice to redeem us from sin. It is important to know that these scriptures have remained intact and untarnished (cf. chapter 2), and they contain the very messages God wants us to know.

Through Jesus

About two thousand years ago, when the time was just right, God spoke in an entirely new way: He spoke through His Son and created a new covenant with humanity. This was His plan developed before the creation of the world (Ephesians 1:2–14). He spoke through Jesus and continues to speak to us through Jesus today when we pray and when we read the Word. Because Jesus was with God and came from God, His teachings reflect the very heart, mind, and purposes of God. "In the past God spoke to our forefathers through the prophets at many times and in various ways, but in these last days he has spoken to us by His Son, whom he appointed heir of all things, and through whom he made the universe" (Hebrews 1:1–2). The coming of Jesus was a pivotal point in the history of the world. It changed the direction of the world and is responsible today for who you are and the culture in which you live. Our study will examine the evidence that Jesus was the Son of God, the Savior of the world, who is coming again and is who He said He was. Of all the things to know with certainty, knowing Jesus is the most important.

Through Creation

On any dark night, look into the heavens and God is non-verbally speaking to you through one of the most awesome sights on which our eyes can focus. Similarly, see the images of an electron microscope that looks at things so small we cannot see them with the naked eye or a standard microscope. Study the orderly and precise interaction of life-giving molecules and processes of living organisms that seem to shout of an intelligence behind them, and God is speaking again. Many of these sights are beyond classical scientific explanations, but science has led us to them, and often only one explanation makes sense: God! The Apostle Paul made note of this: "For since the creation of the world God's invisible qualities—his eternal power and divine nature—have been clearly seen, being understood from what has been made, so that men are without excuse" (Romans 1:20). Time and again one hears the stories told by missionaries who have served in faraway, uncivilized corners of the earth where there have been no Bibles or teaching and preaching, no TV and no Internet. Yet among the tribal peoples there is often an inner sense of a creator God and often a basic code of ethics among them similar to our Ten Commandments.

Words are hard to find to describe the awesomeness and the sovereignty of God creating everything down to its finest detail. In our study you will learn to appreciate the detail, for it is the detailed precision that can only speak to a creator and not a random process.

Through Science

It may be surprising to include science, since many people both inside and outside the faith have for centuries perceived science as anti-religion, and vice versa. However, twentieth-century developments in science have led to significant advances in the understanding of creation and evolutionary life processes. Science has forever changed that perception for people who bother to look seriously into it. Scientific observations go so far as to conclude that certain observations leave no alternative but to point to a creator or designer. Chapter 7 will explain in more detail the exquisiteness and preciseness of creation, which reveals to us how God has spoken through science.

Through Prayer

In prayer we talk with God at any time and any place. Prayer is a conversation with God. Jesus prayed often to His Father and thought it important to leave us a model prayer. The very title of this study, *To Know With Certainty*, comes from the prayer of Jesus in John 17. Jesus tells us to pray in His name. The prayer conversation with God is two-way. If we think of prayer as only talking to God, we may miss the most important part— hearing from God. It is when we pause that we hear. When God speaks as a result of prayer it may not be in an audible voice, but He will speak silently into your mind.

Through Other People

God can speak to us through others. At the urging of the Holy Spirit, others can speak into our lives in various ways including actions, conversation, written materials and the arts. The story of the Good Samaritan is an example of an action. Speaking into others' lives can also be as simple as listening to them.

Any time we do unto others as we would desire others to do unto us, we are speaking God's love into them. Speaking through other people would also include preaching and teaching from the pulpit and in the classroom. Paul tells us in Romans 10:17 that "faith comes from hearing the message, and the message is heard through the word of Christ."

Through the Holy Spirit

Because it is last in this list of how God speaks, it does not mean the Holy Spirit is least in importance. In fact, it may be the most important. The Holy Spirit may be the vehicle through which God conveys the other methods into our hearts and minds. We can read the Word and what Jesus said, study creation, pray, serve, and listen to others, but without conviction by the Holy Spirit, they are just intellectual exercises. In John 14:26 Jesus said that the Holy Spirit was sent by God in Jesus' name to teach us all things and to remind us of what Jesus had said. And further, "when he, the Spirit of truth comes, he will guide you into all truth" (John 16:13).

Did Jesus Really Live? If So, Who Was He?

Jesus Christ was a real historical person. An historical person is one who existed and has a record of doing something significant that was recorded. Let's look at the record.

A fact of first-century history is that a large number of the followers of Jesus, the early Christians, suffered extreme persecution and martyrdom.

If Jesus never lived, if the events of his life never happened and everything about him was a total fabrication, how is it that his followers would die for something that never was?

Furthermore, if Jesus never lived, how likely is it that non-Christian historians would record His existence? But they did. Christians consider the Gospels—Matthew, Mark, Luke, and John—as well as the epistles of the New Testament as sacred Scriptures. They also are historical records, which, as we shall see, meet the tests normally applied to historical documents. Nearly all scholars of antiquity—including the three non-Christian historians portrayed below—agree that Jesus was a historical figure. Such a person *must* have lived.

Flavius Josephus (AD 38-97) was the most prominent and most quoted ancient historian. Josephus was a Jewish scholar who had been captured by the Romans and ultimately freed. His most important works were *The Jewish War*, written about AD 75, and *Antiquities of the Jews*, about AD 94. *Antiquities of the Jews* was written from a Jewish perspective, but because Josephus had become a Roman citizen and lived under Emperor Vespasian, *Antiquities* was probably written for a Roman audience. What Josephus wrote concerning Jesus was the following:

"Now there was about this time Jesus, a wise man, if it be lawful to call him a man; for he was a doer of wonderful works, a teacher of such men as receive the truth with pleasure. He drew over to him both many of the Jews and many of the Gentiles. He was [the] Christ. And when Pilate, at the suggestion of the principal men amongst us, had condemned him to the cross, those that loved him at the first did not forsake him; for he appeared to them alive again the third day; as the divine prophets had foretold these and ten thousand other wonderful things concerning him. And the tribe of Christians, so named from him, are not extinct at this day" (Book 18, Chapter 3, 3).

Josephus also mentioned James, the brother of Jesus, and John the Baptist in his histories. Importantly, all three writings by Josephus are consistent with New Testament accounts.

Pliny the Younger (AD 61-c.113) was the Roman Governor of Bithynia, and around AD 112 he wrote to Emperor Trajan seeking advice on how to manage and legally treat Christians, of whom there were many of every age and class. "They were in the habit of meeting on a certain fixed day before it was light, when they sang in alternate verses a hymn to Christ, as to a god, and bound themselves by a solemn oath, not to any wicked deeds, but never to commit any fraud, theft or adultery, never to falsify their word, nor deny a trust when they should be called upon to deliver it up; after which it was their custom to separate, and then reassemble to partake of food—but food of an ordinary and innocent kind" (*Letters* 10.96-97). In this writing, confirming what the New Testament Scriptures report, Pliny describes the worship of Christ as a God and the Christians' effort to live morally and meet together for worship (church).

The writings of **Tacitus** (ca. AD 56 - ca. 117), the Roman historian and senator, parallel the Gospel accounts in his mention of Christ, His crucifixion by Pontius Pilate, and the persecution of Christians in Rome by the Emperor Nero. This is what he reported in his *Annals* ca. AD 116: "Nero fastened the guilt ... on a class hated for their abominations, called Christians by the populace. Christus, from whom the name had its origin, suffered the extreme penalty during the reign of Tiberius at the hands of ... Pontius Pilatus, and a most mischievous superstition, thus checked for the moment, again broke out not only in Judaea, the first source of the evil, but even in Rome ..." (Book 16, Chapter 44).

The New Testament's 27 books are Scriptures, but also first-century historical documents. The physician Luke, writer of the Gospel of Luke and the book of Acts, is considered by many to be one of the earliest foremost historians. He gets this reputation for the detailed accounts of events and his connection to the eyewitnesses to Jesus' ministry. Some of the things he mentioned in his writings were of such detail that they were met with confusion, because he was reporting on things that were unheard of. However, archeological discoveries in recent times have proved him correct and have added to his standing as an historian.

Was Jesus The Messiah and Divine?

This is the most important question for mankind in the history of the world. The question demands an answer because it has eternal consequences. An affirmative answer is the guarantee of eternal life. A negative answer leads to eternal separation from God.

Atheists such as Richard Dawkins dismiss the idea of Christ's divinity:

"The historical evidence that Jesus claimed any kind of divine status is minimal" (Dawkins, 92). But Christians base their affirmative answer on the New Testament itself. Jesus never said the words "I am God." He did say enough to leave no doubt that He claimed to be God and also the Son sent by His heavenly Father. (See the section "What Did Jesus Say About Himself?") It is hard to fathom how the culture in Jesus' time missed the signs of His divinity based on what He did.

What Did Jesus Do to Demonstrate His Divinity?

He Forgave Sins

Mark 2:5—"And when Jesus saw their faith he said to the paralytic, 'My son your sins are forgiven.'" When accused by the Pharisees of blasphemy because only God can forgive sins, Jesus answered them, "But that you may know that the Son of Man[2] has authority on earth to forgive sins ... I say take up your bed and walk" (Mark 2:10-11), and the man was healed. In this one answer there are two statements by Jesus that indicate to the Pharisees that He is God. First, He forgave the man's sins, knowing—as the Pharisees did—that only God can forgive sins. Second, He demonstrated a divine power of healing.

He Healed the Sick

Jesus healed many people, both individually and en masse, from a variety of diseases, including demonic possession. There are numerous reports attesting to Jesus' healings. In Matthew 8 we see two examples. Verses 1-4 give the report of a man healed immediately by the simple touch of Jesus' hand: "When he came down from the mountainside, large crowds followed him. A man with leprosy came and knelt before him and said, 'Lord, if you are willing, you can make me clean.' Jesus reached out his hand and touched

---

[2] The term Son of Man is a way to refer to a special human being that "rides the clouds." In the OT, "riding the clouds" meant deity. Jesus is saying that as Son of Man He is deity. Indeed, Jesus does things as a human that we expect from a deity—like healings, raising people from the dead, etc. (cf. Bock and Wallace).

the man. 'I am willing,' he said. 'Be clean!' Immediately he was cured of his leprosy."

In verses 5-13 we read of Jesus healing the servant of an officer. "When Jesus had entered Capernaum, a centurion came to him, asking for help. 'Lord,' he said, 'my servant lies at home paralyzed and in terrible suffering.' Jesus said to him, 'I will go and heal him.' The centurion replied, 'Lord, I do not deserve to have you come under my roof. But just say the word, and my servant will be healed. For I myself am a man under authority, with soldiers under me. I tell this one, "Go," and he goes; and that one, "Come," and he comes. I say to my servant, "Do this," and he does it.' When Jesus heard this, he was astonished and said to those following him, 'I tell you the truth, I have not found anyone in Israel with such great faith. I say to you that many will come from the east and the west, and will take their places at the feast with Abraham, Isaac and Jacob in the kingdom of heaven. But the subjects of the kingdom will be thrown outside, into the darkness, where there will be weeping and gnashing of teeth.' Then Jesus said to the centurion, 'Go! It will be done just as you believed it would.' And his servant was healed at that very hour."

In both stories, great faith in Jesus' power is shown by those seeking healing. Fifty healings of Jesus have been recorded with their Biblical references (StrongInFaith.org).

He Raised People From the Dead

There are three accounts of Jesus raising people from the dead. Jesus raised the son of the widow of Nain (Luke 7:11-15), and He raised the daughter of Jairus, a ruler of the synagogue (Luke 8:41, 42, 49-55). Most prominent of all is the account of Jesus calling his friend Lazarus from the tomb, recorded in John's gospel.

"Jesus, once more deeply moved, came to the tomb. It was a cave with a stone laid across the entrance. 'Take away the stone,' he said. 'But, Lord,' said Martha, the sister of the dead man, 'by this time there is a bad odor, for he has been there four days.' Then Jesus said, 'Did I not tell you that if you believed, you would see the glory of God?' So they took away the stone. Then Jesus looked up and said, 'Father, I thank you that you have heard me. I knew that you always hear me, but I said this for the benefit of the people standing here, that they may believe that you sent me.' When he had said this, Jesus called in a loud voice, 'Lazarus, come out!' The dead man came out, his hands and feet wrapped with strips of linen, and a cloth around his face. Jesus said to them, 'Take off the grave clothes and let him go'" (John 11:38-44).

He Demonstrated Power over Nature

The gospel stories of Jesus walking on water and calming the Sea of Galilee during a severe storm are examples of a divine attribute of controlling the weather. Other demonstrable examples of power over nature are the previously cited examples of raising people from the dead and His own resurrection from the dead.

What Did Jesus Say About Himself?

Jesus talked about himself and was very direct in the description of His relationship to the Heavenly Father. For example, in the synagogue He was handed the scroll of the prophet Isaiah and read: "The Spirit of the Lord is on me, because he has anointed me to preach good news to the poor. He has sent me to proclaim freedom for the prisoners and recovery of sight for the blind, to release the oppressed, to proclaim the year of the Lord's favor … Today this scripture has been fulfilled in your hearing" (Luke 4:18-19, 21). While not declaring that He is God, Jesus is here saying that He has been appointed by God.[3]

John the Baptist sent a messenger to Jesus and asked, "Are you the

---

[3] Jews do not believe that the messiah will be divine. One of the fundamental differences between Judaism and Christianity is the Jewish conviction that God is so essentially different from and beyond humanity that he could never become a human. Moreover, Jews find no foundation in the Scriptures for such a belief about the messiah. However, the Tanakh (Hebrew Bible, essentially the Christian Old Testament) gives several specifications as to who the messiah will be. He will be a descendent of King David (2 Sam 7:12-13; Jer 23:5), observant of Jewish law (Isa 11:2-5), a righteous judge (Jer 33:15), and a great military leader. Muslims totally reject Jesus as God and reject the concept of the Trinity. To Muslims, Jesus was a prophet and He was Muslim.

one who was to come, or should we expect someone else?" (Mathew 11:3). Jesus replied, "Go back and report to John what you hear and see: The blind receive sight, the lame walk, those who have leprosy are cured, the deaf hear, the dead are raised, and the good news is preached to the poor" (Mathew 11:4-5).

When Jesus came before the Sanhedrin, He was asked, "'Are you the Christ, the son of the Blessed One?' 'I am,' said Jesus. 'And you will see the Son of Man sitting at the right hand of the Mighty One and coming on the clouds of heaven.' Then the high priest tore his clothes, 'Why do we need any more witnesses?' he asked. 'You have heard the blasphemy. What do you think?' They all condemned him as worthy of death" (Mark 14:61-64). To the priest who recited the Shema, "Hear, O Israel: The Lord our God, the Lord is one" (Deuteronomy 6:4), it was not possible to think of God as more than one being, and Jesus' words constituted blasphemy and demanded the death sentence.

In John 10:24-26, 30, Jesus is told by the Jews, "'If you are the Christ, tell us plainly.' Jesus answered, 'I did tell you, but you do not believe. The miracles I do in my Father's name speak for me, but you do not believe because you are not my sheep. I and the Father are one.'" The Jewish leaders understood what he was saying because they replied in verse 33, "We are not stoning you for any of these [miracles] but for blasphemy, because you, a mere man, claim to be God." Jesus concludes his claim to be God's Son by appealing to what the leaders have seen, namely, His miraculous, God-given power: " ...even though you do not believe me, believe the miracles, that you may know and understand that the Father is in me, and I in the Father" (John 10:38).

In John 8:56–59, in response to the Pharisees' question, "Who do you think you are?" Jesus said, "'Your father Abraham rejoiced at the thought of seeing my day; he saw it and was glad.' 'You are not yet fifty years old,' the Jews said to him, 'and you have seen Abraham!' 'I tell you the truth,' Jesus answered, 'before Abraham was born, I am!' At this, they picked up stones to stone him, but Jesus hid himself, slipping away from the temple grounds."

The violent response of the Jews to Jesus' "I AM" statement indicates they clearly understood what He was declaring—that He was the eternal God incarnate. Jesus was equating Himself with the "I AM" name God gave Himself in Exodus 3:14. That is a powerful assertion that thrills us believers, but it was a red flag to the Jewish leaders.

In John 14:9-10, Jesus said to Philip, one of his disciples, "Anyone who has seen me has seen the Father. How can you say, 'Show us the Father'? Don't you believe that I am in the Father, and that the Father is in me? The words I say to you are not just my own. Rather, it is the Father, living in me, who is doing his work.'"

What Did Others Say About Jesus?

The opening lines of the Gospel of John say it all clearly. While too extensive a narrative about Jesus and His relationship with God to dissect here, John 1:1-18 is must reading. Here John, an eyewitness to Jesus, declares clearly who Jesus is: "He was the Word and the Word was God. He was with God in the beginning" (John 1:1).

In arguably the most famous passage in the New Testament, John reaffirms Jesus' identity as the Son of God and the Savior of mankind: "For God so loved the world that He gave His one and only Son, that whoever believes in Him shall not perish, but have eternal life" (John 3:16).

Jesus understood that people wondered who he was. So he asked His disciples, "'Who do people say the Son of Man is?' They replied, 'Some say John the Baptist; others say Elijah; and still others, Jeremiah or one of the prophets.' 'But what about you?' he asked. 'Who do you say I am?' Simon Peter answered, 'You are the Christ, the Son of the living God.' Jesus replied, 'Blessed are you, Simon son of Jonah, for this was not revealed to you by man, but by my Father in heaven'" (Mathew 16:13-17).

Finally, after doubting the Resurrection and on meeting the risen Christ, Thomas acknowledges Jesus' divinity: 'My Lord and My God.'" (John 20:28). Jesus never corrected Thomas; He accepted the title of Lord and God.

Did Jesus Fulfill Prophecy?

Prophecy is a divinely inspired proclamation—speaking God's words, as it were, a revelation—and a prediction, a statement about something that will happen in the future. Prophecy is a significant part of the Bible. The ultimate test of a predictive prophecy is whether the prophecy comes true. Numerous websites have reproduced a list of 44 Old Testament prophecies that were fulfilled by Jesus, and other sites have claimed over 300 prophecies in the Old Testament about the Messiah's coming (Christianity.About.com; see also Appendix A).

Did Jesus Really Rise From the Dead?

The Resurrection of Jesus from the dead is perhaps the most important piece of evidence that Jesus was the Messiah. It is the final proof for those seeking proof. Yet it is probably the most difficult to believe because, outside of Jesus (and Lazarus), has anyone else been resurrected from the dead three days after having been pronounced dead? This may be the most important question of all, and it certainly demands an answer because it is the biggest stumbling block for non-believers. To the Jews questioning his identity, Jesus stated that he would die and that he would rise from the dead: "Destroy this temple [my body] and I will build it up again [i.e. rise from the dead]" (John 2:19).

To have a resurrection, there must be a death, so the first question should be, "Did Jesus really die?" Some skeptics who admit that there may have been an historical Jesus still say that Jesus never died; they even claim that He planned and staged His death and Resurrection. Here are some facts that disprove such claims of a "swoon" or "drugged" state resembling death.

The Romans were experts at execution and particularly crucifixion. Flogging prior to crucifixion was part of the execution process. When Jesus approached the cross, He had already endured flogging with whips made of bone and metal that tore flesh from His body. Often the underlying bone was exposed and people did not survive the flogging. After the flogging, Jesus then carried the cross, probably the 100-pound cross member, to the crucifixion site, which further weakened Him. (If ever there was question about whether Jesus was a man's man, consider His strength that let him endure this flogging and still carry the cross.)

Jesus was placed on the cross and nailed through His wrists and feet with nails about 6 to 8 inches long. The cross was hoisted, and the weight of His entire body was suspended from His hands and supported by His feet. He had to push up with his feet in order to breathe. Slowly he would die an excruciating, painful death by asphyxiation, as the pushing up from His feet would eventually sap all of His energy. (Note that this is where the word "excruciating" comes from—it means "out of the cross.")

Crucifixion was a very efficient method to execute people and involved unimaginable suffering from the scourging alone. Nailing the feet and hands to the cross required all of the weight to be on the feet and the chest would be collapsing in on the lungs as the body sagged. To relieve this the person would push up with the legs to breathe until he no longer could and then death would be slow by asphyxiation. Hypovolemic shock, a loss of blood and bodily fluids, would induce great thirst, tachycardia, pericardial effusion and ultimately heart failure. Heart failure in turn would cause a pleural effusion (a collection of fluid around the lungs that deprives of oxygen) and subsequent asphyxiation. This condition was evident when a Roman soldier thrust a spear into Jesus' right side and up toward the heart; both water and blood flowed out. Jesus was dead at this point.

With the Sabbath approaching, the soldiers wanted to speed up Jesus' death. Normally they broke the legs to speed up death, but when they came to Jesus He was pronounced dead. Thus, His legs were not broken, which fulfilled another prophecy. Remember, the Roman executioners were experts in crucifixion and accountable for successfully carrying out the execution. Not to do so would mean that these Roman soldiers would be punished by death. Jesus was dead.

Lawrence Krauss, a theoretical physicist and high-profile atheist, disputes the idea that Jesus actually rose from the dead. "There are no definitive eyewitness accounts of these events, and in the case of the claimed resurrection the scriptures were written decades after the claimed event, and the different accounts are not even consistent. Isn't it more likely that those who were preaching to convert fabricated a resurrection myth in order to convince those to whom they were preaching of Christ's divinity?" (4-4-2016). This statement is conjecture with its use of words like "definitive" and "likely" and is typical of people who have not examined the evidence and like to push forward a worldview hidden beneath their declarations that have no factual basis.

As usual, those who argue against the Resurrection do not accept any evidence from the Bible and can offer no counter evidence of their own. In spite of their brilliance in their chosen field, it is as if they are blinded, as described in Scripture. Commenting on those who had witnessed Jesus' miracles and yet refused to believe in Him, John writes, "For this reason they could not believe, because, as Isaiah says elsewhere: 'He [God] has blinded their eyes and deadened their hearts, so they can neither see with their eyes nor understand with their hearts … '" (John 12:39-40). Or as Paul put it, "The god of this age has blinded the minds of unbelievers, so that they cannot see the light of the gospel of the glory of Christ, who is the image of God" (2 Corinthians 4:4).

The first evidence for a resurrection was the empty tomb. No one has refuted the claim that the tomb was empty. When no body could be produced, a number of conspiracy theories were spawned. Even Jesus' disciples were skeptical when first told by the women who went to the tomb that He had appeared to them. The disciples had disregarded what He told them before His death, that in three days He would arise. His followers did not anticipate seeing him again. They were in hiding, fearing for their lives, until He appeared to them in the Upper Room.

Let's examine some of the objections: Could the body have been stolen? Matthew reports that there were guards at the tomb, and that makes sense. People were aware of Jesus' claims, and the Jewish leaders would have been wise to place guards so the body would not be stolen. The Jewish leaders would not steal the body themselves, for that would only perpetuate the claim of Resurrection.

Then there is the question of the tomb being open. Archaeologists report that a stone sealing a tomb would usually sit in a carved-out slot on such an angle that it rolled downhill on closing. Opening the tomb would require several men pushing the stone uphill, a daunting task that would not go unnoticed by the guards. The disciples would be the only ones with a conceivable reason to steal the body, namely to make it look like Jesus had fulfilled his own prophecy, but consider this:

+ To steal the body they would have had to overcome a contingent of Roman guards;
+ It is not likely the guards were asleep, because doing so would have invited their own execution;

- The linen cloths used to cover Jesus' face and body were left folded at the tomb. Would someone stealing the body really have taken the time to do that?
- The biggest consideration: would a disciple commit himself to a life of persecution, extreme suffering, and ultimate martyrdom if he knew He had faked a Resurrection? Many deluded people die willingly for a false idea that they believe to be true; no one dies willingly for something he knows to be false.

Another conspiracy theory without proof is that Jesus escaped and went to a foreign land. Another theory claimed He was drugged (speculating that the sponge of hyssop cited in Mark 15:36 contained a sedative) and only fainted. But knowing what we do about a Roman crucifixion—the scourging, the beatings, the loss of blood, the asphyxia, and the sword thrust into His side releasing the pleural effusion—it would be ludicrous to conclude that Jesus could have fainted and escaped.

Eyewitnesses are always evidence in a court or a debate, and the recorded appearances of the resurrected Jesus, such as in the Gospel of Luke and the Book of Acts, are key evidence. One of the most effective testimonies, however, might be the Apostle Paul's in 1Corinthians 15:5-8. Consider the series of witnesses that Paul records: Jesus first appeared to Peter, as mentioned in Luke 24:34, then to the disciples, eleven in number at that point, as in Luke 24:36. Then Paul says that Jesus appeared to more than 500 people, most of whom are still alive. The implication here is that the reader of Paul's letter can seek out those witnesses to verify the story—"Go ask them yourself!" he seems to be saying.

Three more evidences follow. James, the half-brother of Jesus, was a skeptic himself but later a Christ-follower. Then there is another mention of all the Apostles, as recorded in Luke 24 and Acts 1, and finally Paul's emphatic first-person testimony: "last of all he appeared to me also, as to one abnormally born" (1 Corinthians 15:8). Even though Paul was not one of the original twelve disciples and had not met Jesus before the Resurrection, he was "born" or grafted into their band after his encounter with Christ on the road to Damascus.

In light of the collected testimonies of encountering the risen Christ, those who reject His Resurrection cannot provide any evidence that Jesus did *not* rise from the dead. Everything that they offer is only a denial and rejection of any evidence in support of the Resurrection.

There is a final point concerning the disciples and the Resurrection. Picture Jesus hanging on the cross, dead, bloodied, emaciated, and looking nothing like the leader they had followed. Having witnessed miracle after miracle, they would have expected Jesus miraculously to prevent His death. They were discouraged and probably wondered whether they had been duped. What had not yet registered to them was that He came to die and be resurrected, overcoming death as an example to them. If they believed in the Resurrection, they too would live forever. Would they have gone on to risk their lives and suffer at the hands of persecutors for a myth or fabrication? No! The Resurrection was the seminal event that made them willing to die for their belief. Ask yourself: if you had seen what they had seen, could anyone ever talk you out of it? Would you not go to extreme lengths, including persecution and death, as an advocate for the person who did this?

The eyewitness evidence for Jesus and His Resurrection has been well documented. It is important to know the details of the Resurrection and its defense. The best narrative is *The Case for the Resurrection of Jesus* by Gary Habermas and Michael Licona.

The next question to ask is, what about the trustworthiness of the documents? Let us see how they fit the criteria required of ancient documents to be accepted as true.

CHAPTER 2

Is the New Testament True?

"Then you will know the truth, and the truth will set you free." John 8:32

The New Testament is God's latest covenant with His people. It is the second major part of the Christian canon that we call the Bible. The first part of the Bible is the Old Testament, which is based on the Hebrew Bible. The New Testament, originally written in Greek, discusses the teachings and person of Jesus, as well as events in first-century Christianity. Christians regard both the Old and New Testaments together as sacred Scripture. The New Testament reflects and serves as a source for Christian theology and morality. Our Christian church services today range from the orthodox liturgical to the less liturgical, and they incorporate readings from the Old and New Testaments. The New Testament has influenced just about every aspect of life for generations, including religious, philosophical, and political movements. It has been the subject of countless works of literature, art, and music. Its advocates have been some of the most famous people of all time. Without Christianity there would be no Western civilization as we know it.

Can the Gospels be Trusted?

If Christianity is to be trusted as a true religion, the New Testament must be trusted to have accurately reflected the birth, life, death, and Resurrection of Jesus and the work of His disciples after He was gone. If Christianity cannot be trusted, then the greatest hoax of mankind has been perpetrated. The latter is often what humanists believe and want you to believe, and many times students on college campuses have been confronted with such a view. While Christianity has grown to be the world's largest religion at about 2.2 billion adherents, the followers of Jesus Christ have been persecuted for their faith since Christianity began. The persecution has been worldwide and has been violent to the extreme. In America, a country founded by Christians on Christian principles, that persecution has taken on a battle for the mind and soul of people.

For much of the twentieth and now twenty-first centuries, there has been a concerted attempt to discredit Christianity. The attack has been led by an atheism that permeates our educational and political systems from people in positions of power and influence. They will challenge every aspect of Christianity from the events reported concerning Jesus' life and Resurrection from the dead to the authorship and authenticity of the New Testament. These challenges do not treat the information found in the New Testament as factual accounts by writers who were eyewitnesses and who were willing to die for their beliefs. Modern skeptics, reflecting a revisionist history and theology, are typically found in the university and even in some churches.

One prominent academic, Bart Ehrman, challenges the validity of Scripture and the process of formulating an orthodox faith: "Here is how Christianity really began," writes Ehrman. "There were lots of early groups. They all claimed to be right. They all had books to back up their claims, books allegedly written by the apostles and therefore representing the views of Jesus and His first disciples. The group that won out did not represent the teachings of Jesus or His apostles. Rather, the victorious group called itself orthodox, but it was not the original form of Christianity and won its victory only after many battles" (DVD).

Chris Hallquist, president of "Atheists, Humanists and Agnostics" at UW-Madison, discounts the eyewitness nature of much Scripture when he writes, " …in the eyes of almost all informed non-Christians, and many more liberal Christian biblical scholars, the Bible contains *no* eyewitness reporting on Jesus' life … The authors of the New Testament could *easily* have been just writing down legends about Jesus, and there's good reason to think in many cases they were" (July, 2012).

These statements have an impact upon an eager-to-learn student not fully equipped to deal with the statements. The charges made in these statements regarding the New Testament and the first-century church claim an information gap, fabrication, distortion, embellishment, mythology by informed non-Christians and scholars who should know better. Let's look at all of these as we learn about the facts that support the truthfulness of the New Testament.

It is time to ask the question, "If the New Testament is true, would you be a Christian?" If the New Testament is true, you have been offered the greatest deal of all time. In Chapter 7 we will see that the almighty God, creator of the universe, has gone to unimaginable lengths to assure you a place in eternity for reasons known only unto Him. Therefore, it is of paramount importance that you consider this deal. Just like a business deal, God's offer is dependent on you agreeing. What is different about this deal is that God has already laid out his side of the deal, and it is very one-sided in your favor. However, it is non-negotiable; it is a free gift. You only need to take it, but taking it requires an act of faith that the deal is true. Some people have difficulty accepting this free gift because they do not believe it.

The terms of the deal have been laid out in the New Testament, and in this section we can examine them to see if they look trustworthy. To assess the terms, we need to rely on the same methods used to prove that George Washington was the first President, or the first permanent English settlement was at Jamestown, Virginia in 1607. These methods are based on historical documentation and supported through archeological discoveries. While history and archeology cannot be repeated as in a science experiment, they can through writings and artifacts constitute evidence that the events happened. They are still not 100% proven—you would have to have been there as an eyewitness to be 100% sure. However, when we read the writings of people who lived during Jamestown or when Washington was President, we receive eyewitness evidence and get a lot closer to 100% in believing that these events happened. Similarly, when we read the documents associated with the settlement at Jamestown and dig up the earthen remains of the Jamestown fort, we know there was a fort there. So it is with "proving" Christianity—we must rely on evidence that can be uncovered.

Another factor that enters in when we talk about events that cannot be 100% proven is interpretation. For example, we know George Washington regularly attended the Anglican Pohick Church in Virginia and that he was a church official. His religious status has been debated: was he a Christian or a deist? Here we get into beliefs, usually on the part of the person exploring or teaching the topic. Someone who is a deist may want to prove Washington was a deist. When I read what Washington said about Christianity, I believe he was a Christian. So when it comes to Christianity, much will ultimately depend on what you decide to believe. It is a choice that you have to make based on the work of the Holy Spirit and your own investigation.

When we say we know with certainty that "God so loved the world that he gave his one and only Son, that whoever believes in him shall not perish but have eternal life" (John 3:16), we cannot prove it 100%, but we cannot disprove it either. Weigh the evidence and make a decision to believe, then confidently commit to it. Once that decision and commitment are made, your life is altered. I believe that you will agree— the evidence speaks for itself and enhances your walk with God through Jesus.

Did the New Testament Writers Engage in Fabrication?

When I was a child, I enjoyed listening to my elder family members describe some event to which they were eyewitnesses. Invariably, there would be different recollections of the details of the event, but never disagreement on whether the event took place. So it was with the first-century writers. They may have had differences in recalling those events, and maybe more so for events that they did not witness, such as Jesus' birth. However, the Scriptures exist to answer charges of fabrication made by today's skeptics because they remind us several times, sometimes in several places, of the things to which they *were* eyewitnesses.

Peter, for example, speaks for his fellow Apostles when he assures readers that his writings are reliable: "We did not follow cleverly invented stories when we told you about the power and coming of our Lord Jesus Christ, but we were eyewitnesses of his majesty" (2 Peter 1:16-18).

The Apostle John likewise assures readers of his Gospel that he not only witnessed the works of Jesus, but also wrote them down for posterity: "This is the disciple who testifies to these things and who wrote them down. We know that his testimony is true" (John 21:24).

And while Luke the physician and historian is forthright enough to admit that he was not an eyewitness of Jesus, he also assures us that his "orderly account" is based on "eyewitnesses and servants of the word."

Furthermore, he has "carefully investigated everything from the beginning," so that his readers "may know the certainty of the things you have been taught" (Luke 1:1-4).

A charge of fabrication leveled at the New Testament writers is ludicrous for another reason, beside the eyewitness reports: every Apostle writer in the New Testament endured extreme persecution and suffering, and all except John were martyred for their faith. Had the stories been fabricated, the writers might have been labeled lunatics but not martyred for something demonstrably false.

There is more evidence that would counter the charge of fabrication. For example, in the culture of the time, women would likely not have been accepted as credible eyewitnesses in a scriptural narrative, yet we see in Luke 24:1-2 that women are announced as the first witnesses to the Resurrection. If one were inventing this story and trying to "sell" it as truth, women would never have been cited as eyewitnesses, because the story would lack credibility. Yet they *were* cited, because that is what happened. It spoke to the truth. The story was "not for sale."

Another example is the empty tomb and the events surrounding the Resurrection. Recall the discussion "Did Jesus Really Rise from the Dead?" in Chapter 1.

What Was the "Information Gap"?

Christianity arose from a group of followers of Jesus after His Crucifixion and Resurrection from the dead in Jerusalem about AD 30. This group was composed of the 12 Apostles and hundreds if not thousands of disciples (followers). These Apostles, who were Jesus' inner circle, and other disciples spread the good news (gospel) throughout the then known world from Jerusalem to Spain and England. The facts supporting the events and process are true and supportable by biblical and historical documentation.

It is acknowledged by both Christian and non-Christian scholars that what is called an "information gap" existed between when Jesus lived and when the New Testament was written. There is general agreement among New Testament scholars that the 27 books arose between approximately AD 50 and the AD 90s. There was a gap of at least 20 years between Jesus' life, death, and Resurrection in AD 30 and their earliest recording by eyewitnesses in AD 50-55. During this time, however, a solid oral tradition kept alive the stories of Jesus.

Certainly, the more time there is between when events happen and when they are recorded, the greater the potential difficulty in recalling them. However, some critics have exaggerated this time frame, placing the initial 20-25-year gap at 40 years and even suggesting that some New Testament writings originated as late as the second century. Such a long time, they argue, would make it impossible for the oral testimony among Jesus' followers to accurately reflect the events of His ministry. There was, they claim, sufficient time for fabrications, distortions, and inventions to arise in the oral tradition. Dating the writing of the Scriptures so far out from the events, contrary to documented data, is an obvious attempt to discredit their authenticity. Such a view does not take into account other information from reliable biblical and non-biblical sources that challenge this time frame. Rather, the evidence points to a continuity of information leading to a truthful and authentic New Testament.

A common phrase used today in intelligence circles and in crime investigations is "connecting the dots." It means to arrive at a conclusion by creating a chronology of events based on available facts and evidence. When it comes to the truths of the Christian faith, we can indeed connect the dots beginning with Jesus.

It is important to remember that the so-called "information gap" was not an information *void*; rather, the 20-25 years were a period of preaching, active discussion, and remembrances of the events with fellow eyewitnesses. While the Jerusalem and Damascus disciples were going about the Great Commission Jesus had left for them—to make disciples and baptize them—Paul and his followers were preaching and teaching based on information gleaned from eyewitnesses and personal contact with the risen Christ. As Paul reports, "For what I received I passed on to you as of first importance: that Christ died for our sins according to the Scriptures, that he was buried, that he was raised on the third day according to the scriptures, and that he appeared to Peter, and then to the Twelve. After that, he appeared to more than five hundred of the brothers at the same time, most of whom are still living, though some have fallen asleep. Then he appeared to James, then to all the apostles, and last of all he appeared to me also, as to one abnormally born" (1 Corinthians 15:3-8).

In this passage Paul is saying, in effect, 'I received the information I am telling you from others, eyewitnesses, as well as my own conversion experience. Furthermore, what I received concerning Christ's sacrifice for our sins, his burial, and his Resurrection was also in line with the Scriptures.' In citing the Scriptures, Paul might be referencing Old Testament prophecy that had been translated into Greek in the Septuagint, or he may have been citing earlier New Testament writings that are not available to us but may have been relied upon by the authors of the four Gospels.

Paul's writings need a special examination because of when they were written, what information was available to him at the time, and how the information likely came to him. This is important, because it speaks to the continuity of the information and how the dots can be connected. Paul had persecuted the Christians, including the martyred Stephen, for the very things he now claimed to be true. His presence at Stephen's stoning in about AD 32 would also suggest that Paul would be of such an age that he may have known about Jesus and His ministry during His lifetime. In other words, Jesus and Paul overlap, making Paul an eyewitness of sorts. As Paul stated in 1Corinthians 15:3-5, he had access to Scriptures.

The turning point for Paul was his conversion experience in about AD 32 through a personal encounter with Jesus on the road to Damascus recorded in Acts 9. That in itself is evidence of the life and death of Jesus, because Paul, a highly-educated and well-connected man for his time, gave up a very good position and probably a promising career to commit his life to what he knew to be true. His commitment was so strong that he endured hardship, suffering, persecution, and ultimately death.

Shortly after his conversion, Paul began to meet and work with the early church leadership in Damascus and in Jerusalem (Acts 9:19-20). He had ongoing interaction with Peter, James, John, and the other disciples, all eyewitnesses to the events surrounding Jesus. The Book of Acts is Luke's historical documentation of the Apostles' activities in the first few years after Jesus had gone to be with the Father. It is clear from Acts that Paul was working with eyewitness information before he wrote 1 Corinthians, considered by some scholars to be the first NT writing in AD 55. This is a span of about 20 years following Paul's conversion and 25 years following the Resurrection of Jesus. From reading the book of Acts, one can see that the early community of believers was very active and serious about the mission Jesus had given them.

It is reported in Galatians 1:12-17 that Paul left Damascus to go into Arabia where he encountered the risen Christ who revealed the Gospel to him before Paul made contact with the disciples in Jerusalem. This was within a few years of his conversion, placing the Gospel information he received only five years after Jesus' Resurrection. The fact that some scholars consider Galatians to have been the first of his letters in 50-55 AD makes it contemporary with that of the Gospel writers. The fact that Paul never took issue with the four Gospel writers, including Luke, who was one of his traveling companions, provides confirmation of the truthfulness of the events.

Paul's writings take on new importance when viewed in this context because, while he did not write specifically on the events of Jesus' life, he did write on His death and Resurrection in a confirming manner. The Scriptures teach that Jesus taught and performed extraordinary miracles before thousands of eyewitnesses, many of whom also witnessed His death and Resurrection. After Jesus' Resurrection, as we have shown, there was no information void but rather a continuous stream of information passed from Jesus to the Apostles and disciples. The timeline below summarizes for you the sequence in which that information was documented in the books that comprise the New Testament.

New Testament Timeline

AD 30	AD 32	AD 33	AD 50-55	AD 60	AD 62	AD 90s
Crucifixion & Resurrection. Pentecost, Apostles' teaching	Paul's Conversion	Paul begins ministry	Paul writes Galatians & First Corinthians	Matthew, Mark, Luke, Acts written	Paul Martyred	John writes his Gospel, 1,2,&3 John, and Revelation

20-25 Year Gap

What Were the Sources for the Four Evangelists?

The sources of information for the four Gospels were a combination of eyewitnesses and earlier manuscripts since lost. Because of the close association of the disciples as they went about their respective missions following Pentecost, they must have continuously discussed the events of Jesus' life with each other, which would provide a basis for reliability of the information.

Mark is known to be the first of the four Gospels, and his work was known to Matthew and Luke. Collectively these three books are known as the Synoptic (=seen with one view) Gospels. However, because there are sayings in two of the books not found in the third, many scholars believe that another source was used by Matthew and Luke that was not known to Mark. (That hypothetical source has been labeled "Q," from the German word *Quelle*=source). While that theory takes nothing away from their writings, it must be remembered that Mark, the first Gospel writer, had a close association with Peter, the other disciples, and with Paul. As we will see later, Paul mentions that he was aware of Scriptures, meaning there were perhaps other documents in circulation in addition to Q.

John's writings in the AD 90s are different than the synoptic Gospels. The Gospel of John stresses Jesus' relationship with God and says that He is God, the Way, the Truth, the Life, and the Resurrection. Very likely John saw no need to write what the others had written.

It is clear from the opening words of Luke's Gospel that he is acting as an historian to record the extraordinary events of Jesus life and resurrection. His attention to cultural and governmental detail of the time has been corroborated by other historical works and has been commented on favorably by Bible scholars. In addition, Luke lived at a time when surviving Apostles like Peter, James, John and perhaps other eyewitnesses were available as resources. This is akin to sitting down with World War II or Pearl Harbor survivors in the 1950s or 60s and getting first-hand accounts of what happened in the 1940s.

In the years between Jesus' death and the writing of New Testament books, the Apostles were busy going about their mission of fulfilling the Great Commission. While their primary means of communication would have been oral, the message did not require the usual oral transmission from one generation to another before being written down. Instead, the writings were all done in the lifetime of the eyewitnesses and those who knew them. To take a modern example: consider talking today to the people involved in the 9/11 tragedy. If there were no existing media coverage, you could still piece together a reliable story of what happened 15-20 years ago.

29

As noted by Paul in the 1 Corinthians 15 passage cited earlier, there was a lot of communication between the Apostles and disciples, and the Book of Acts describes the interactions among them. These interactions would add to the accuracy of their writings as they discussed events and verified the stories among themselves. This point is neglected when skeptics state that so much information could be lost in the years between when the events happened and were reported in Matthew, Mark, Luke, and John.

The power of personal contact among and between the eyewitnesses and Paul was significant. The evidence of their lives would indicate that their communications were not subject to corruption as they were passed along, such as happens in the party game variously called Telephone or Whisper Down the Lane. It is clear from Acts that Paul, Peter, James, John, Luke, and Mark all had very close associations and would have discussed the happenings frequently.

Remember, they went to their deaths convinced that Jesus' death and Resurrection had given them eternal life. Put yourself in their shoes: you are following a man with whom you have had personal contact for three years and whom you believe to be the Son of God. You have seen his miraculous powers, and even though he has predicted his death, you are shocked and dismayed when all of a sudden he is killed. They could not lift a finger to prevent it. He has been killed by the greatest military power on earth and with the public aid of your own religion's leaders. For three days they hid in fear because they might kill them too. Suddenly He appears before them, having risen from the dead. They have personal contact with Him for forty days. They see Him ascend into heaven, and ten days later they are present when the Holy Spirit of God that He promised would come descends on them at Pentecost. No wonder they risked their remaining lives for such a being and considered Him God.

Are the New Testament Documents Authentic?

The truth claims of the New Testament are supported, first, by the reports of *eyewitnesses*, many of whom were willing to die rather than recant, and, second, by the *short gap* of time between the historical events and their recording in our Scriptures. A third criterion for establishing the veracity of the New Testament is the *reliability of the copies* we possess.

While there are no original complete manuscripts of the New Testament, there are sufficient copies and a high degree of inerrancy in the copies that would render the Scriptures authentic. It is important to scholars involved with documents of antiquity to know how many copies of an ancient manuscript exist. The more copies there are, the more credible the original document. When the copies are consistent with each other, this means there was little modification from the earliest texts.

How do the Gospels compare to other ancient manuscripts in terms of numbers of manuscripts? Consider these statistics of established classics and compare them to what we have of biblical texts:

Ancient Manuscripts	# Found	Originals
Homer's Iliad	643	None
Sophocles	193	None
Aristotle	49	None
Livy	20	None
Caesar's War Commentaries	10	None
Tacitus	10	None
Herodotus	8	None
Plato's Tetralogies	7	None
New Testament	24,000	None

Note the overwhelming number of biblical manuscripts, which include over 5,664 in the original Greek and 18,000 portions of the New Testament in other ancient languages (Bierle, 30-31).

How Close Are the Manuscripts To the Actual Events?

As described earlier, the closeness of the earliest manuscripts to the actual events is very important. The longer the gap between when copies were made and when the original was written, the greater the possibility exists for errors, deletions, and additions. The earliest NT writings are the John Rylands papyrus, dating to about AD 125, which contains a few verses of the Gospel of John. Since John was writing around AD 90-100, the writer of the papyrus could actually have known John. There are also the Bodmer Papyri (the books of John, Jude, and 1 & 2 Peter) from about AD 200, and the Chester Beatty Papyri (texts of the Gospels of Matthew, Mark, Luke, and John) dating from AD 120-150. These manuscripts, preserved in museums in the United Kingdom, are excellent testimony to the accuracy of the biblical copies that followed. They also show an interval of only about 60-100 years between the original writings and the oldest surviving copies. Now compare that gap with the other ancient manuscripts that we routinely accept:

Manuscript	Interval (years)	Date of Original
New Testament	100	50-100 AD
Virgil	300	
Homer	500	800 BC
Caesar	950	50 BC
Tacitus	1000	116 AD
Plato	1260	
Herodotos	1350	
Aristotle	1450	(Bierle, 33-34)

Again in the words of Don Bierle, "the Gospels were in written form very early. They did not go through a long period of oral transmission during which they took on legendary traditions. No other ancient writing can trace its manuscript copies all the way back to the generation of the eyewitnesses and its original authors!" (33).

How Sure Are We About The Authors Of The New Testament?

Bart Ehrman claims that the four Gospels cannot be attributed to the four authors indicated in the New Testament because there are no surviving original manuscripts that identify the authors. However, the absence of an original manuscript does not void the attributed authorship, because there is documentation from the Apostolic Fathers—early church leaders discussed in more detail in Chapter 3—that the authors attributed to the Gospels are correct. The Apostolic Fathers reported having direct interface with the disciples who were eyewitnesses to the events recorded in the Gospels. Thus, the early church testifies to Matthew, Mark, Luke, and John as authors.

There is some confusion about the Gospel of John because it is not clear among some scholars whether John the Apostle or John the Elder was the writer. However, in John 21:20-24 it says that John the Apostle wrote the book. Papias (AD 60-130), Bishop of Hierapolis in Asia Minor (present-day Turkey), knew John and was a companion of Polycarp, who was also a disciple of John. Papias affirmed in AD 125 that both Mark and Matthew had written their Gospels. Papias also testified to Mark's accuracy when he wrote that Mark "made no mistake" and did not have "any false statement." Papias, quoting the Apostle John, also wrote, "Mark, having been the interpreter of Peter, wrote down all that he said, whether sayings or doings of Christ, not, however, in order" (cf. Lovell).

Irenaeus (AD 130-220) was a student of Polycarp, who was a student of the Apostle John. In *Against Heresies* Irenaeus stated, "Matthew published his Gospel among the Hebrews in their own tongue when Peter and Paul were preaching the Gospel in Rome and founding the church there. After their departure [death], Mark, the disciple and interpreter of Peter himself handed down to us in writing the substance of Peter's preaching. Luke, the follower of Paul, set down in a book the Gospel preached by his teacher. Then John, the disciple of the Lord, who leaned on his breast, produced his own Gospel while living at Ephesus in Asia." Irenaeus further stated, "So firm is the ground upon which these Gospels rest, that the very [heretics] bear witness to them, and starting from these documents, each one of them endeavors to establish his own particular doctrine" (311).

In the second century Justin Martyr (100-165 AD) showed a deep familiarity with Matthew, Mark, and Luke by quoting from them extensively and, while not mentioning the Gospels by name, referred to them as "Memories of the Apostles." He quoted also from John.

Paul's letters leave little doubt that Paul was the author. It is generally accepted that the authorship of the New Testament is as in the following table:

The New Testament and its Authors

Writer	Book
Matthew	Matthew
Mark	Mark
Luke	Luke Acts
John	John I John II John III John Revelation
Peter	I Peter II Peter
James	James (Jesus' brother)
Jude	Jude
Paul	Romans Philippians I Timothy I Corinthians II Corinthians Colossians Titus I Thessalonians II Thessalonians Philemon Galatians Ephesians
Undetermined	Hebrews*

*Scholars no longer attribute Hebrews to Paul. Some believe the epistle was written by Barnabas; others suggest it was Apollos.

What about Additions to Scripture?

In the Gospel of Mark chapter 16, verses 9-20 appear to have been added because two of the oldest manuscripts, the Codex Sinaiticus and Codex Vaticanus, do not contain them. Because older and more accurate manuscripts do not have the verses, it is concluded that the original Mark did not have them. However, the addition does not change the Scripture's meaning. One can also discover about 17 other verses throughout the Gospels that are not present in all available translations. Often there is a footnote to explain that some earlier manuscript did not have this language. The added or missing passages are usually only a sentence or clause within a sentence and have little bearing on the Gospel as a whole. Some appear to have been added for clarity or emphasis. Skeptics will say that these differences are conflicts. Some may sound like conflicts but really are simply differences in recollection. **None of the missing verses have theological consequences.**

Why Are There Sometimes Different Descriptions of the Same Event?

There are a number of different descriptions of the same event in the Gospels, and accounting for these differences requires some research. It is important to recognize and admit the differences, but equally important to explain how these differences would have come about.

When encountering passages labeled conflicts by the skeptic, you will notice that they usually do not include the explanation for the differences offered by Christian scholars. And often the skeptic accuses the early Christian writers of intentionally falsifying or fabricating events. It is tempting to list the textual differences and the skeptic's claims, followed by the Christian explanation, but that would require a very lengthy exercise that would go beyond the scope of this book.[4]

If every Gospel were a verbatim copy of the others in describing the

---

[4] For a detailed analysis of textual differences in the Gospels and their translations, as well as a full analysis of skeptics' comments, see Hank Hanegraff, *Has God Spoken? Proof of the Bible's Divine Inspiration.*

same event, the writers would be accused of collusion or alteration to make an exact look-alike copy. The fact that they are not verbatim says something about the integrity of the Gospel writers and those who assembled the New Testament. But anticipating that you might be challenged sometime on this point, let's look at a couple of examples of textual differences that do not constitute misrepresentation of the historical events.

Some differences require an understanding of the writers' perspective. For example, when was Christ crucified? Mark states that Jesus was crucified the 3rd hour, and John states that He was standing before Pilate at the 6th hour. How could He stand before Pilate after He was crucified? The explanation lies in the time or clock used in reporting the event. Mark, using Jewish time, which begins the day at 6:00 a.m., has Jesus being crucified at the 3rd hour, or 9:00 a.m. in Roman time. John using Roman time, which, like our time begins at midnight, had Jesus before Pilate at the 6th hour or 6:00 a.m. and crucified three hours later, at 9:00 a.m., just as Mark stated. There is no conflict.

The different genealogies of Jesus provided in Matthew and Mark are another example. Skeptics have had a field day with the different genealogies as a reason to proclaim that Jesus was not the Messiah, yet none of the skeptics' scenarios are based on fact. Scholars state that Matthew's Gospel provides the genealogy through Joseph's line and Luke's through Mary's line. Even though Joseph was not Jesus' biological father, his line is reported by Matthew, a Jew, because it was customary in Jewish genealogies to report the father's line. Scholars believe Luke was a Gentile Christian and physician. Because of this, he may not have felt compelled to report the paternal line but instead the maternal line, since he recognized that Joseph was not the biological father. Both genealogies speak of Jesus' birth to Mary and report that she is a virgin. The fact that the genealogies are not exactly the same suggests that Matthew and Luke did not get together and compare notes to make sure they were saying the same thing. They just saw it differently.

How Accurately Were New Testament Manuscripts Copied?

In making copies there is room for error, and accuracy is vital to acceptance by scholars of ancient manuscripts. Here are three scholarly testimonials to the overall accuracy of New Testament manuscript copies. First, Don Bierle compares the rate of distortion—defined as differences affecting the reader's understanding, not spelling or word order changes—in the NT and two other ancient documents. The table below shows that the Bible has virtually no significant distortion due to copying error (Bierle 35).

A Comparison of the Rate of Distortion of Manuscripts Due to Copying Errors

Manuscript	#Lines	#Distorted Lines	Distortion Rate
New Testament	20,000	40	0.2%
Iliad	15,600	764	5%
Mahabharata	250,000	26,000	10%

Second, Norman Geisler and William Nix write, "The New Testament, then, has not only survived in more manuscripts than any other book from antiquity, but it has survived in a purer form than any other great book—*a form that is 99.5 percent pure*" (cited in Strobel, 85).

Finally, Dr. Bruce M. Metzger, a longtime professor at Princeton Theological Seminary and one of the most influential New Testament scholars of the 20th century, explains that the variants existing in NT manuscripts are insignificant for two reasons: 1. the way they are counted. For example, one word misspelled the same in 2,000 copies is counted as 2,000 variants. 2. the doctrinal insignificance of the variants. "I don't know of any doctrine that is in jeopardy. None ... The more significant variants do not overthrow any doctrine of the church" (cited in Strobel, 84f.). Asked whether investigating the variants in ancient biblical manuscripts has affected his faith, positively or negatively, Dr. Metzger testifies, "It has increased the basis of my personal faith to see the firmness with which these materials have come down to us, with a multiplicity of copies, some of which are very, very ancient ... I've asked questions all my life, I've dug into the text, I've studied this thoroughly, and today I know with confidence that my trust in Jesus has been well placed. *Very* well placed" (cited in Strobel, 93).

When someone tries to discredit your faith in the reliability of the New Testament manuscripts, remember these words of a brilliant scholar like Dr. Metzger who spent a lifetime digging into the texts and asking the tough questions about them. His trust in Jesus was *very* well placed indeed, and yours can be too!

CHAPTER 3

How Did the Christian Church Develop?

You do not need to know church history in great detail, but you should know enough to recognize what the church, despite some of its failures, has done positively to arrive at where it is today. In particular, there should be an appreciation for the many reformers that kept the faith and theology consistent with first-century intentions.

Challenges to faith will come in the form of criticisms from non-believers who are anti-church for many reasons too numerous to go into here. They will rely on hearsay, without any consideration of how historically documented events contributed to the church and its Christian ministry. Your goal is to have at least an appreciation of what went on in the church to meet the goal Christ had for it.

In this chapter we will see how a series of seemingly coincidental historical events may have been orchestrated by a God who wanted them to happen for His very specific purpose, the salvation of the world. Also, you need to recognize that not all of church history has been pretty or Christ-like; there are reasons for that, and you should know and acknowledge them. You should also be able to explain the good that came through reformers who stood up for the faith. Opponents of the church, assuming they know at least some church history, will focus on the negative events, but you need to remember this: the church grew over the last 2,000 years because it was good and offered something to mankind that the world had not previously known.

Good news (*Gospel* in Greek) spreads fast, and the small world we know today as Israel and the Mediterranean area had never received such good news. The news was that "God so loved the world that he gave His one and only Son, that whoever believes in him shall not perish but have eternal life"

(John 3:16). The long-expected Messiah had come, and this was the news He brought. This was the best deal mankind had ever received, one planned by God before the creation of the world to make men holy and acceptable in His sight through Jesus (cf. Ephesians 1:2-14).

The Good News was received initially by people who came to know it with certainty, and they knew it with such certainty that they were willing to die for what they knew. The actions of the Apostles and their disciples, and the disciples of the disciples, are the most powerful evidence of the truth of the Good News. Looking back 2,000 years from today, it is hard to put ourselves in their place and feel the fervor over what they had witnessed, but that fervor was sufficient to facilitate the spread of the Gospel throughout the Mediterranean world. There is not enough space here to cover in detail all of the events used by God to fulfill His purpose for saving mankind from eternal damnation, but what follows should give you a useful overview.

What Were Some Major Pre-New Testament Events?

What Was the Diaspora?

The Old Testament speaks of four Diasporas of the Jewish people. Looking back on them it is easy to see how they figured into God's plan to develop and grow the church. *Diaspora* is derived from a Greek word meaning "dispersion" or scattering of a people group from its homeland. Sometimes the dispersion has been a mass migration and at other times a trickle of people over a long period of time. Some dispersion has been voluntary to escape a certain way of life, and some has been removal by force. There have been many dispersions in history, even into present times, and significant changes in world history have occurred because of various mass migrations of people.

The four Jewish Diasporas were the result of invasion and occupation of the homeland in Palestine, and they would logistically serve God's purpose. The first dispersion followed the Assyrian invasion from 740 to 722 BC that resulted in the displacement of thousands of Hebrews. This displacement was of the ten tribes of the Northern Kingdom, called Israel, which was an area corresponding to today's Israel, Lebanon, and Syria. They were dispersed throughout the Assyrian kingdom, an area that covered modern-day western Iran, Iraq, and southeastern Turkey. These tribes are referred to as the Ten Lost Tribes, so called because they were assimilated into other cultures, where most lost their Jewish identity. The Assyrian empire subsequently fell to the Babylonians, setting the stage for the next dispersion.

The second exile was in 597 and 586 BC when Judah, the Southern Kingdom, fell to Babylon's King Nebuchadnezzar. The Judahites were taken captive as a group into Babylon (modern-day Iraq) but not assimilated as in the case of the Assyrian invasion. They remained there until Babylon fell to King Cyrus of Persia in 539 BC, at which time they were allowed to return to Jerusalem to rebuild the Temple in 538 BC. Not all returned, for even today there are descendants of these people in Iraq and Iran. Later, when the Greeks in the fourth century BC (3rd dispersion) and the Romans beginning in 63 BC (4th dispersion) controlled Palestine, many Jews fled, eventually scattering over the Middle East and North Africa.

Collectively, the Diasporas were essential to the spread of the Gospel message. At the time of Jesus' death on the cross around AD 30, Jews were firmly entrenched around the Mediterranean and throughout the Middle East, having instituted their own customs and religious traditions in local synagogues. These synagogues constituted a network that would greatly aid in delivering the coming Gospel. This spread of the Good News, in response to the command of Jesus in Matthew 28:18-20, is covered in the Book of Acts, as well as in the Apostle Paul's epistles and the writings of the Apostles Peter and John.

How has God used the Diaspora? First, He allowed His chosen people, even as they were exiled, to take monotheism and His Word beyond the Promised Land into areas of polytheism and paganism. Second, after the birth of the church at Pentecost and the fall of Jerusalem in AD 70, Jewish Christians and other converts, using the marvels of Greco-Roman civilization and communication, took the Gospel throughout the known world and ultimately westward as far as Spain and western Europe.

What Was the Septuagint?

Growth was also influenced by other events preceding the first century. The Septuagint was a translation of the Old Testament from Hebrew into Koine Greek, the language of the day. Ptolemy II, king of Egypt, asked seventy-two

Jewish scholars to do the translation in the early third century BC, and it was completed in the second century BC. The Septuagint contained the Hebrew Bible and other related texts. Because many early Christians spoke and read Greek, they now had access to an Old Testament that they could read for themselves in a language they understood. Interestingly, the books of the Septuagint were in the approximate order that, when later combined with the New Testament, is the order of the Bible we have today.

How Did Roman Culture and Infrastructure Help the Church?

Also assisting in the growth of the church was the Pax Romana, featuring the Roman contribution of roads, aqueducts, and law that allowed a free flow of commerce and travel faster and over longer distances. This enabled news and information to spread faster, and the Gospel message was no exception. This may not seem significant today given our instantaneous information media, but 2,000 years ago it was very significant. The establishment of this infrastructure by the Romans before Jesus came is an example of how God works in the affairs of men to make human events serve His plan.

What Was the Common Language?

By the beginning of the first century, the Diaspora had resulted in a Jewish population sprinkled among Gentiles in Turkey, Greece, Macedonia, and probably as far away as Spain. In modern-day terms, a network had been established. For the network to be more effective, it required a common language.

As a result of the conquests of Alexander the Great around 330 BC, the Hellenistic culture significantly influenced the region of Palestine up to and through the Roman occupation. The Hellenistic influence was culturally broad, liberalizing fundamental Judaism, embracing the use of debate for new ideas, and contributing to the arts and literature, so that the general populace became better educated.

The area had been undergoing a transition in language from its earliest times of Hebrew to Aramaic and then to Greek. As Greek became the language of commerce and writing, it was particularly adopted by the Gentiles. The twelve Apostles would have spoken Aramaic and Hebrew and may have had some familiarity with Greek. This was significant, because the Apostle Paul, who was fluent in both Hebrew and Greek, was able to target Gentiles for the Gospel message throughout the Christian outposts. The conversion of the Gentiles, as we will see later, was a game changer for the world. The Greek language was an important ingredient in God's plan; it became the literary language of the New Testament as it had earlier in the Septuagint (cf. Fitzmyer). As a common language for a network of believers, it spread the Gospel through Palestine, modern-day Syria, eastern Iraq, Turkey, Southern Italy, the Greek isles, and pockets of coastal North Africa and the Black Sea.

What Were Some Major First-Century Events?

What Was the Birth of the Christian Church?

After the birth and Resurrection of Jesus, the most important event in the New Testament is the event we call Pentecost. Fifty days following Passover, is the day of Pentecost, a Jewish holiday known as the Festival of Weeks and ordered in Leviticus 23:9. It was a time when Jews would have been in Jerusalem, and as recorded in the second chapter of Acts, what happened that day was a trigger that changed the world.

The Holy Spirit is reported as descending on a gathered crowd of about 120 believers on the day of Pentecost. As a result of what happened, Pentecost is considered the birth of the Christian church. That day the believers were filled with the Holy Spirit, and they began to speak in other tongues understandable to the many "God-fearing Jews from every nation under heaven" (Ac 1:5) who were present. Many of these people were descendants of the earlier Diaspora. They were reported to be from Parthia, Medes, Elam, Mesopotamia, Judea, Cappadocia, Pontus, Asia, Phrygia, Pamphylia, Egypt, Libya, Rome, Crete, and Arabia. The incident at Pentecost resulted in 3,000 people being baptized. These believers returned to their homes as no longer singularly Jewish but as Jewish Christians. The synagogues in their cities and towns would become outposts that the Apostle Paul, being Jewish and now also Christian, would later visit to preach the Gospel. They, along with the Apostle Paul, would become the first New Testament missionaries of a changed world.

It was through this early church[5] that the Gospel spread, and this was according to God's plan. In Ephesians 3:10 the Apostle Paul tells us that God's intent was that through the church His manifold wisdom would be made known throughout the realms of the heavens and to all known powers and authorities. God's purpose, planned before the creation of the world, was to make all who believed in him through Jesus Christ holy and blameless in His sight (Ephesians 1:2-14). John, Peter, and the other Apostles were the early leaders. Countless others would remain true to the founding purposes of the church and keep it marching forward as God's instrument on earth. These people are today's cloud of witnesses that can be added to those listed in Hebrews 12. We owe them much for keeping and maintaining the Scriptures intact for us.

The first-century church was devoted to prayer, preaching, evangelism, and writing. The writings would become the New Testament canon if the writer could be traced to eyewitness accounts going back to Jesus' life, death, and Resurrection. The church grew significantly during this time, in spite of intense persecution by the Romans and by the Jewish establishment. It was Jewish converts to Christianity who initially made up a church that was considered a Jewish sect, but as the Gentiles were added, church growth gained in momentum.

The early church appealed to Jewish and Gentile converts, who accepted Christianity for the following reasons:

- the power of the Holy Spirit on them;
- the moral direction Christianity offered to a morally depraved Roman Empire;
- the equality and respect it offered;
- the personal relationship with God it offered;
- the fact that circumcision was not required for Gentiles.

---

[5] For this discussion, the word "church" will mean a community of believers and not a denomination or established institutional church. The institutionalized church failed at different times in history when church leadership abandoned the mission that God had set for them. These failures came as a result of the church leadership focusing on its power and being involved in political objectives, rather than serving the people. These acts wounded the church in ways that are felt today.

What Was the Didache?

There is an ancient document I want to introduce to you. It has been very meaningful to me because of when it was written and how theologically consistent it is with what we believe and what we practice at church today. It is important enough to me that I want to pass it on to you. Examining it is well worth your time.

The Didache (DIH-da-key or -kay) has been dated by one scholar to AD 40-60, which places it at the time of Paul and Mark's Scripture writings, maybe before (Cross, 482). Some scholars think it may have been circulated as early as AD 60. The Didache refers to Matthew, Luke, and 1 Corinthians, indicating that these works were in circulation when it was written. The anonymously written Didache is considered the oldest surviving example of non-canonical literature. Its authorship is unknown, and it was discovered in 1873.

The subtitle of the document in one translation is *"The Lord's Teaching Through the Twelve Apostles to the Nations."* It is a testimony of the early church fathers, many of whom had direct lines of communications back to Jesus and the Apostles. The Didache is like a catechism and presents a first-century view of Christian ethics, the sacraments of Baptism and Holy Communion, and how to be a follower of Jesus. The Didache was considered a manual for pastors, relating how Jewish Christians adapted Judaism for the gentiles. Its revelations in this regard are greater than in any other Christian writing. Interestingly, the practices described in the Didache are the same as today, which strengthens the argument that first-century practices and theology were kept intact by believers down through the ages.

Who Were the Apostolic Fathers?

Jesus had chosen His 12 disciples who, after Pentecost, also made disciples, some of whom became founders of the late first and early second-century churches. These men were known as the Apostolic Fathers, the early church fathers mentioned above in Chapter 2. They had been face-to-face with the eyewitnesses, so oral tradition or direct communication had been passed down reliably. Apostolic Fathers were important links in the chain of information that continued the eyewitness accounts. They also served another important function: defending the faith against false teachings and heretical sects that had no biblical basis. As we consider several of them, do you see the clear connections back to Jesus?

- **Clement of Rome (d. AD 95)** was a first-century convert, taught by Peter or Paul. He became Bishop of Rome, the fourth pope. According to Tertullian, Clement was ordained by Peter. He is considered to be the first of the Apostolic Fathers.
- **Polycarp (AD 80-167)** was a second-century Bishop of Smyrna (modern Turkey). A disciple of John and companion of Papias, he was martyred in Rome for refusing to recant his faith.
- **Ignatius (ca. AD 50-117)** was an auditor of John and third Bishop of Antioch (in modern Turkey). He was martyred for his faith in the persecution by Emperor Domitian.
- **Papias (AD 60-130)** was bishop at Hierapolis (modern Turkey). He was the earliest to write about the Gospel's origins. Papias sought out eyewitnesses to Jesus or people in contact with eyewitnesses. He affirmed in AD 125 that Mark and Matthew had indeed written their Gospels. Papias testified to Mark's accuracy when he wrote that Mark "made no mistake" and did not have "any false statement."
- **Irenaeus (ca. AD 125-202)** was bishop in Gaul (modern France) and a student of Polycarp. In his five-volume work *Against Heresies*, written in AD 180, he bears solid witness to the authorship of the Gospels and challenges heretical sects such as Gnosticism.
- **Tertullian (AD 150-240)**, from Carthage in North Africa, was also a vigorous defender of the faith against heresies such as Gnosticism. His extensive writings in Latin helped give that language prominence over Greek in theological literature.
- **Augustine of Hippo (AD 354-430)**, though two centuries later than the others, was one of the most important of Church Fathers. His thinking on grace, salvation, the Trinity, and original sin and his writings such as *The City of God* and *Confessions* profoundly influenced the development of Western Christianity and philosophy.

In addition to being men of responsibility in the early church, these leaders were in a good position to say what early writings were true. Because of their contact with the eyewitnesses, they had much to say about who wrote the four Gospels. Their writings support the authenticity of the New Testament texts.

A surviving written testimony from Clement confirms the role of the Apostles: "The Apostles received the Gospels for us from the Lord Jesus Christ. Jesus Christ was sent from God. So then Christ is from God and the Apostles are from Christ. Both therefore came of the will of God in the appointed order. Having therefore received a charge, and having been fully assured through the resurrection of our Lord Jesus Christ and confirmed in the Word of God with full assurance of the Holy Spirit, they went forth with the glad tidings that the kingdom of God should come. So preaching everywhere in country and town, they appointed their first-fruits, when they had proved them by the Spirit, to be Bishops and Deacons unto them that should believe" (Clement 1, 42).

Consider again the skeptic's claims that, because there are no surviving original manuscripts, we cannot ascertain the New Testament authors with assurance. The absence of originals does not void the attributed authorship because there is documentation from the Apostolic Fathers, who had direct connection to the eyewitnesses, that the authors attributed to the Gospels are correct.

Hebrews 11, often called "the faith chapter," holds up earlier heroes of the faith as models for New Testament Christians, and Hebrews 12:1 encourages them to carry the faith into the future: "Therefore, since we are surrounded by such a great cloud of witnesses, let us throw off everything that hinders and the sin that so easily entangles, and let us run with perseverance the race marked out for us." This the Apostolic Fathers have done for us, providing not only a chain of unbroken information but also a model for running the race of life with perseverance.

What Were Some Major Second to Fourth-Century Events?

As noted above, the Apostolic Fathers were active in furthering and maintaining the faith during the second to fourth centuries. In addition, this period saw an expanded church, a divided church, and new beliefs that required the attention of church leaders to avoid a permanent schism. It was during this period that Eusebius (AD 263-339), the Greek bishop of Caesarea Maritima, wrote the first history of the church that survives to this day and has become a reference to all histories thereafter.

During this period Gnosticism—a dualistic sect that saw matter as evil, spirit as good, and salvation as available through secret knowledge—was a persistent challenge to Christianity. Gnosticism predated Christianity and was not Christian; however, its writings during the second century were influential in some circles. The early church leaders opposed Gnostic influence on Christianity, and no Gnostic writings were included in the New Testament. The Gnostic gospels, as they are called, should not be confused with the New Testament Gospels, for the Gnostic gospels were not divinely inspired. In fact, some were written as much as several hundred years after the New Testament Gospels. A great debt is owed to the early church fathers who opposed the Gnostic heresy.

In AD 292 a significant event occurred that would lay the groundwork for a major split in the church, the effects of which are felt to this day. The Emperor Diocletian divided the empire into eastern and western halves, which later under Constantine placed the capitals in Byzantium (later to be named Constantinople, and Istanbul today) and Rome. Division of the empire also had the effect of dividing the church into eastern and western halves.

In AD 313, the Edict of Milan by the Emperor Constantine legalized Christianity after more than 200 years of persecution and set the stage for the Council of Nicaea (AD 325) and the Nicene Creed. Sandwiched between these events was the Arian controversy that threatened to split the church; Arianism, as it was called, believed that Jesus was not fully God. It was because of Arianism that the Council of Nicaea was convened by Constantine. The Council was a showdown of sorts, and from it emerged the church's embrace of the doctrine of the Trinity and Jesus' full divinity.

What Was the Core Theology of the Early Church?

The Didache along with the first-century NT Scriptures reflect a first century core theology that has survived the years. This core theology was passed down through the writers and copyists for the first 200 years, from

Jesus to the Apostles to the disciples of the Apostles and successively on to later church fathers. That is not to say that there were not some differences in interpretations during the early years but the church sorted through them. The theology was ultimately expressed in the Nicene Creed (AD 325, rev. 381) and the Apostles' Creed (2nd -3rd century, in present form since 650), which are recited today in churches all over the world. The basic doctrines of church theology today were rooted in the earliest of churches and originally called the Rule of Faith. While each church had its own Rule of Faith, each of them also retained the basic elements of the core theology. This is significant because it speaks to a continuity of the theology from the beginning to today. While there may be different denominations today, each with its own story of development, the core theology has prevailed.

The consistency of the core theology was a reason for church growth. The aforementioned Irenaeus was one of the Apostolic Fathers who advocated for adherence to the original theology. He believed that only traditions handed down through the succession of elders from the eyewitnesses should be adopted as doctrine. In *Against Heresies*, the five-volume work written in reaction to unbiblical sects, he crafted a statement of faith that echoed the Trinitarian principle of Matthew 28:17 and stressed the importance of church unity: "The church, though dispersed throughout the whole world, even to the ends of the earth, has received from the apostles and their disciples this faith in one God the Father Almighty, Maker of heaven, earth, and the sea and everything in them; and in one Christ Jesus, the Son of God, who became incarnate for our salvation; and in the Holy Spirit. As I have already observed, the Church, having received this preaching and this faith, although scattered throughout the world, yet, as if occupying but one house, carefully preserves it. She also believes these points just as if she had but one soul and one and the same heart" (I:10:1). In reading Irenaeus, one can see the seeds for the Nicene Creed, which became official some 200 years later in AD 381. Importantly, the core theology was developed in the first two centuries and was maintained by Apostolic Fathers like Irenaeus to provide us with the core theology we have today.

The Good News (Gospel) spread fast, and there were mass conversions of people from all corners of the Middle East as both the Apostles and their converts spread the message. By AD 180, the time of Irenaeus, the entire Mediterranean and parts of Europe and England had received the Gospel.

This was done not with military conquest but by preaching, teaching, and reading the writings of the Apostles, and it was fueled by the power of the Holy Spirit and the presence of extreme persecution. As Irenaeus explains, "For the churches which have been planted in Germany do not believe or hand down anything different, nor do those in Spain, nor those in Gaul, nor those in the East, nor those in Egypt, nor those in Libya, nor those which have been established in the in the central regions [i.e., the Middle East] of the world. But as the sun, that creation of God, is one and the same throughout the world, so also the preaching of the truth shines everywhere and enlightens all men that are willing to come to a knowledge of the truth" (1:10:1-2).

What Were Major Fifth-Century to Seventeenth-Century Events?

The division of the church by Emperor Diocletian in AD 292 led over time to a growing friction between the eastern and western halves. This was accompanied by increasing church powers, blurring the division between church and state. In AD 410 Rome fell to the northern barbarians, and the church, as a remaining institution, filled the power vacuum, gaining still more influence. Over the ensuing years there remained a fragile unity between the Eastern Orthodox and Roman Catholic churches. That unity was forever shattered, and a final schism came in 1054. In 1204 an event occurred that was a significant turning point, not only in church history but in world history.

From 1099 to1204 a series of Christian Crusades were launched against the Middle East. Since AD 638 the Muslims had controlled Jerusalem and all access to it. Christians believed that a pilgrimage to Jerusalem was an indication of their faith, much like Muslims believe in the pilgrimage to Mecca. The Muslims had been harassing Christians and forcing them to pay large tariffs to make the pilgrimage. In 1099 Pope Urban II delivered an influential sermon urging the removal of the Muslims from the lands previously held by Christians in Palestine. The Pope promised forgiveness of sins for those who would make the pilgrimage and destroy the "infidels." The First Crusade was underway, funded by several European landowners. They met in Constantinople and proceeded to Jerusalem where they slaughtered Muslims, Jews, women, and children in a bloody massacre.

This event would have far-reaching consequences on how Jews and Muslims would perceive Christians in the future.

This was the last victorious Crusade, as the Muslims later retook Jerusalem and repelled the Second and Third Crusades. The Fourth Crusade (1202-1204) was also a failure and a glaring blemish on the church that remains to this day. The Fourth Crusade never reached the Holy Land. Instead, because of a financial obligation necessary to fund it, the Crusaders stopped in Constantinople, where they dethroned the Eastern emperor and raped, pillaged, and tortured the eastern Christians. The damage was so bad that the Eastern Church never fully recovered, and the incident remains a low point in Christian church history. The Eastern Church and Byzantine Empire were so weakened that they were no match for the invading Ottoman Turks in 1453. Constantinople, now called Istanbul, which occupies a strategic place on the Bosporus Strait, has forever since been in Muslim control. The Crusades, though initially prompted by Muslim aggression, ultimately became a blemish for the church on an otherwise sterling record of accomplishment in fulfilling God's mission. The Crusades serve as example of what happens when a personal relationship with God through Christ is replaced by other competing relationships such as power and corruption.

The Crusades were not the only example of church leadership and power going terribly wrong from AD 1000 to 1500, and all in the name of Christ. There were also the abuses of indulgences, church division, power plays, and inquisitions that burned fellow Christians alive at the stake because they disagreed with the direction of the church. These offenses came from the church assuming the role of governments and being influenced by greed, money, and power, where the people's needs were secondary. Basically, the church abandoned the role that God had set for it in Ephesians 3:10, "that now, through the church, the manifold wisdom of God should be made known to the rulers and authorities in the heavenly realms."

The events of this period are often cited today by non-believers as a reason for not embracing the faith. We need a response for this, because the church was doing many good things, without which we would be different today. The response is that what non-Christians consider to be the church was merely the flawed institution. The real church was a community of believers, sinners saved by grace, many of whom were active reformers addressing the shortcomings of the institutional church. We owe much to these reformers who kept the theology. They are our modern-day cloud of witnesses.

To focus only on the abuses is to overlook the many positive influences of the church, for example in education. Since the 300s the church had set up schools to educate its people. These were often attached to a cathedral, and some grew into university-level education for the clergy. The education was not only religious—it also included, law, science, and philosophy, such as the ancient teachings of Plato and Socrates. The availability of the Scriptures coupled with the classical education enabled these students to see philosophy, law, and science in terms of Christian ethics. Thus, they came to see the church as a body that should be serving Jesus Christ and not some centralized earthly human power. In some ways, we can say that these are the faithful who saved the church from itself after the Middle Ages and put it back on track, often, like the early church martyrs, giving their lives in the process.

- **Thomas Aquinas (1225-1274)** was an Italian priest considered one of the greatest philosophers and theologians of the Roman Catholic Church. Aquinas combined the medieval system of Scholasticism, which stressed the authority of the church fathers, with the philosophy of the classical philosophy of Aristotle. In his major work, the *Summa Theologica,* he sets forth the well-known "Five Proofs of God's Existence." In 1323 he was canonized as St. Thomas Aquinas.
- **John Wycliffe (1324-1384)** was a dissident English priest, philosopher, and professor best known for creating in the 1300s the first translation of the Bible into English from the Latin Vulgate. In his opposition to church and political hierarchy, he made many enemies, but in his insistence on Scripture as the highest authority for faith, he was a precursor to the reformers of the 15th and 16th centuries. Wycliffe's name lives on in the extensive evangelical enterprise called Wycliffe Bible Translators.
- **Jan Hus (1369-1415)** was a Czech Roman Catholic priest who was an admirer of John Wycliffe. For his critique of church doctrines,

Hus was burned at the stake as a heretic. He was a prominent Protestant reformer a century before Martin Luther.

+ **Martin Luther (1483-1546)** was a German Augustinian monk whose challenge to certain practices and teachings of the Catholic Church, such as the sale of indulgences as remission for sin, triggered the Protestant Reformation. After posting in Wittenberg, Germany his 95 Theses debating the issue of indulgences, and refusing to recant, he was excommunicated by Pope Leo X and condemned as an outlaw by the Emperor of Rome. Luther taught that salvation and eternal life are not earned by human works but are a free gift of God's grace through faith in Jesus Christ. Martin Luther's great literary work was his translation of the Bible into German, which standardized the language and gave people the opportunity to read Scripture in their own language.

+ **Ulrich (Huldrych) Zwingli (1484-1531)** was a prominent leader of the Swiss Reformation movement in Zurich. Like Luther, Zwingli believed in the sole authority of Scripture, but when the two reformers met, they could not agree on the nature of the Eucharist. Zwingli died in a battle with Swiss Catholic cantons.

+ **William Tyndale (1494–1536)** was a British scholar best known for his translation of the Bible into English from both Hebrew and Greek texts. Unwelcome in England, he carried out his work on the European continent and smuggled his Bible into England. Betrayed in the Netherlands, he was executed by strangulation and burned at the stake. Not long after Tyndale's death, his Bible was accepted in England and later became the basis for the famous King James Bible of 1611.

+ **Menno Simons (1496-1561)** was a priest in the Netherlands who initially did not know the Bible. When he began to study it, he found he could not accept some teachings of the Catholic Church because they were not in the Bible. After renouncing the priesthood, Simons embraced the teachings of the Anabaptists, who hold that the church should only baptize believers, not infants. He also taught pacifism and the principle of loving one's enemies. Menno Simons' followers became known as Mennonites.

+ **John Calvin (1509-1564)** was a French pastor and theologian during the Protestant Reformation. After religious strife in France, he moved to Geneva, Switzerland and wrote his landmark *Institutes of the Christian Religion*, which included commentaries on books of the Bible and other theological documents. "Calvinism," which includes the doctrines of predestination and the absolute sovereignty of God in salvation, is foundational for Congregational, Baptist, and Presbyterian churches.

These saints, this great cloud of witnesses to the modern age, lived at the dawn of the Age of Discovery when European countries began to explore far-off lands for their gold and other resources. In doing so, they brought the Christian faith with them and not only colonized the West but also spread the Gospel through the colonies. The expeditions provided the means to get to these lands, but the faith they brought gave them law, order, and eventually freedom. This is how Western Civilization and America were formed. Unfortunately, many colleges and high schools no longer have Western Civilization in their curriculum. If they do, it is devoid of the faith story that accompanied these Christians and provided the foundational principles for the United States of America. In many classes, the history being taught is revisionist history aimed at advancing worldviews that are counter to that of Christianity.

Chapter Four will focus on the Christian contributions to Western Civilization, without which you would not be reading this book.

CHAPTER 4

What Is Your Spiritual DNA?

Did Christianity Help Create Western Civilization?

What was so special about the theology surrounding the Christian faith that led to Western Civilization and the United States of America? From AD 400 over the next 1,600 years until today, it was the orthodox (right) theology that was maintained by key people in the church. Many of these people were the reformers who led the reformation of the church when it stumbled, and stumble it did at different times. In every case, the church survived and became stronger from the inside out, not from the outside in.

Western Civilization is represented today by the modern culture of Western Europe and North America, and various writers have named the following as the major historical influences of Christianity on Western Civilization:

1. The classical culture of Greece (a democratic form of government; the arts and sciences) and Rome (a republican form of government; law and language);
2. The Enlightenment (emphasis on reason and science);
3. The influence of the Christian Church (sanctity of the individual believer; obedience to a higher ruler than emperor or king; separation and limitation of powers) (Stark, 1-2).

Modern Christian writers such as Alvin J. Schmidt, Dinesh D'Souza, James Kennedy, and Cheryl L. Stansberry have documented well the positive influence of Christianity on Western Civilization. Even Bart Ehrman, an atheist and skeptic of early New Testament testimony whom we met in Chapter 2, concedes that the Christian Church has been the most powerful religious, political, social, cultural, economic, and intellectual institution in the history of Western Civilization, from late antiquity to the Middle Ages, the Renaissance, the Reformation and into modern times (#6577).

One of the major contributors to Western Civilization was the university, especially as developed by the Roman Catholic Church. The church has had a long history with education, its first university being established in Bologna in 1088 (Pinsent, 5-6-11). Without Catholicism there would have been no Western Civilization. By the time of the Reformation in 1517, the church had established 33 of the 81 known universities (Woods, 12-28-2011). The great church reformers mentioned in the previous chapter were all products of the educational system of the time. Church clergy were among the better educated of the day, and the Jesuits made significant contributions to the scientific revolution (Woods, 12-28-2011).

Church emphasis on learning was also evident in the cathedral schools that made education accessible to all social classes. In addition, there were the monasteries established to train the clergy. From the fifth century onward, they spread all over Western Europe. By 1500 there were no fewer than 37,000 monasteries belonging to the Benedictine order, sufficient evidence of the important public function of religious orders. If we grant that only one- twentieth of these 37,000 monasteries had regular schools, they would still constitute no small part of the school system of the time (Willmann-Kirsch, 199-200). There were secular schools as well, but the rise of the Christian schools provided an alternative that also taught the Christian religion. Education was not limited to boys; girls had their convents.

The Christian churches would later be the primary force behind the founding of America's universities and colleges. Of the first 108 schools in America, 106 were founded on the Christian faith. Among them, and the oldest, were Harvard, William and Mary, Princeton, Yale, Dartmouth, Columbia, Brown, and Rutgers.

Christianity also promoted liberty and justice, which were generally lacking in non-Christian society, as Alvin J. Schmidt has noted: "The liberty and justice that are enjoyed by humans in Western societies and in some non-Western countries are increasingly seen as the products of a benevolent, secular government that is the provider of all things. There seems to be no awareness that the liberties and rights that are currently operative in free societies of the West are to a great degree the result of Christianity's influence" (248). History is replete with examples of individuals who acted as a law unto themselves, "often curtailing, even obliterating the natural rights and freedoms of the country's citizens" (249). Christianity's influence, however, set into motion the belief that man is accountable to God and that the law is the same regardless of a person's status. "More than one thousand years before the birth of Christ, Moses enjoined the Israelites not to execute anyone for an alleged capital crime without the testimony of at least two witnesses ... This biblical requirement became a vital component of the principle that 'no man is above the law'" (249). The role of witnesses has been adopted by Western nations in administering justice, but it has its roots in the Bible, in the words of Moses in Deuteronomy 19:15 and in the words of Christ in Matthew 18:15-17.

Recognition of and respect for the law has been part of biblical truth since Moses first received the Ten Commandments from God, but the Bible also teaches that the law was known to men because it was written on their hearts; they conducted themselves according to it, even though they had never read the law (Romans 2:14). This means that, through reason and understanding, the law was natural to man. This is similar to stories told by missionaries serving native tribes in areas of the world where there has been no contact with Western Civilization. These indigenous peoples had no written laws for their community, but they understood that laws were necessary for the tribe to survive and bring order to their micro society. Amazingly, their unwritten laws closely paralleled the commandments given to Moses. Their laws were natural to them.

In our Declaration of Independence the existence of natural law is cited as a reason why America was entitled to be separate from England. It says, "When in the course of human events, it becomes necessary for one people to dissolve the political bands which have connected them with another, and to assume among the powers of the earth, the separate and equal station to which the **Laws of Nature and of Nature's God** entitle them, a decent respect to the opinions of mankind requires that they should declare the causes which impel them to the separation" (emphasis added).

Before the Declaration, another document written by Christians in

England had significant impact on the law. Written in 1215, the Magna Carta invoked the name of God in its preamble: "John, by the grace of God …" It further stated that the Magna Carta was created because of "reverence for God and for the salvation of our soul and those of all our ancestors and heirs, for the honour of God and the exaltation of the Holy Church and the reform of our realm, on the advice of our reverend [church] fathers." The document had four points that influenced law. They were: "(1) justice could no longer be sold or denied to freemen who were under the authority of barons; (2) no taxes could be levied without representation; (3) no one would be imprisoned without a trial; and (4) property could not be taken from the owner without just compensation" (Schmidt, 251).

Almost 500 years later these principles would find their way into the Declaration of Independence and the Constitution of the United States. Since the Reformation and the founding of America, Christianity has been intimately involved with our society. Today we seem to have forgotten the influence of Christianity on the founding of America. We do so at our peril.

Is America a Christian Nation?

This is indeed a key question that young Christians will need to understand, as it has been raised by two very public personalities. First, none other than the President of the United States, Barack Obama, who in 2006 declared, "Whatever we once were, we are no longer just a Christian nation."

Television personality Bill Maher of "Politically Incorrect," who is often outspoken against Christianity, goes even farther, claiming "America has never been a Christian Nation." I do not agree with Mr. Maher about many things he says, but in this case he is correct, though maybe not for the reason he thinks. Consistent with his antireligious stand, Maher intended to delegitimize Christianity, but in reality America has never been a Christian nation in the sense of the church governing the country; nor has it ever had an established state religion, to which by law people were expected to adhere in every respect. In the Middle Ages, the Catholic Church was close to being a state religion when in 1302 Pope Boniface VIII affirmed his authority over all spiritual and temporal powers, i.e. including kings. This lasted one month. A modern example of state religion exists in Islamic areas where caliphates exercise Shariah law. And in Scandinavia the Lutheran Church is installed as the "state church" or "people's church," though other faiths are tolerated.

The closest America ever got to a state religion was during the 17ᵗʰ and 18ᵗʰ centuries in Colonial America. Under British rule, the Anglican Church was the state-supported religion in the colonies. Had independence from England not been achieved, the state Anglican Church would have lasted longer. After the American Revolution, the Anglican faith was replaced by the Episcopal faith, but it was not a national religion, because that was prohibited by the First Amendment to the Constitution. Even so, America had been populated by many other Christian denominations, beginning with those seeking religious freedom.

The Christian roots of America trace back to the time before the ships set sail for Virginia. The people who attempted to settle at Roanoke Island in present-day North Carolina in 1585 and 1587 (the inhabitants later disappeared without a trace), the people who later did found the first permanent English settlement at Jamestown, Virginia in 1607, and the Pilgrims who settled at Plymouth, Massachusetts in 1620 were all English Christians. As passengers they came on discovery voyages to escape religious persecution because they were driven by a passionate belief in freely exercising their faith. It is instructive to read the charters establishing the settlements at Roanoke Island and Jamestown, as well as the Mayflower Compact, to see the settlers' missionary goals and their reliance on God for provision and protection.

Among the earliest documents on the settlement of America is the *Instructions for the Virginia Colony* of 1606, issued before the colonists left England. In the second paragraph it says, "When it shall please God to send you on the coast of Virginia, you shall do your best to find a safe port ..." The concluding paragraph says, "Lastly and chiefly the way to prosper and achieve good success is to make yourselves all of one mind for the good of your country and your own, and to serve and fear God the Giver of all Goodness, for every plantation which our heavenly Father hath not planted shall be rooted out." These passages establish that God was in the minds of the people, and they were instructed to serve and fear God and to establish plantations with God's help.

Another document, *The First Virginia Charter* of April 10, 1606, authored by King James and beginning, "James, by the grace of God," goes on to announce the Christian underpinnings of the colonial venture. It was, he wrote, "to deduce a colony of sondrie of our people into that parte of America commonly called Virginia, and other parts and territories of America either appertaining unto us or which are not nowe actuallie possessed by anie Christian prince or people, …" and " …by the providence of Almightie God, hereafter tende to the glorie of His Divine Majestie in propagating of Christian Religion to suche people as yet live in darkness and miserable ignorance of the true knowledge and worshippe of God and may in tyme bring the infidels and savages living in those parts to human civilitie and to a settled and quiet governmente …" It is clear that the Charter was declaring a trust in God and a Christian missionary purpose.

Fourteen years later, on November 11, 1620, *The Mayflower Compact* was signed by 41 of the 102 passengers aboard the Mayflower. Thirty-seven of these were Separatists fleeing religious persecution in Europe. The Compact stated, "In the name of God, Amen. We, whose names are underwritten, the Loyal Subjects of our dread Sovereign Lord, King James, by the Grace of God, of England, France and Ireland, King, Defender of Faith, etc. Having undertaken for the Glory of God and Advancement of the Christian Faith, and the Honour of our King and Country, a voyage to plant the first colony in the northern parts of Virginia; do by these presents, solemnly and mutually in the presence of God and one of another, covenant and combine ourselves …" They were pledging in the name of God and had as a purpose to advance the Christian faith in the New World, though they expected to do that in Virginia, not in Massachusetts, where they landed.

Later, on May 19, 1643, the *Articles of Confederation* between the plantations under the Government of Massachusetts, New Plymouth, Connecticut and New Haven was drawn up for the purpose of uniting the Puritan colonies in support of the church, and for defense against the Native Americans and the Dutch colonies of New Netherland. In the lead sentence it states, "Whereas we all came into these parts of America with one and the same end and aim, namely, to advance the Kingdom of our Lord Jesus Christ and to enjoy the liberties of the Gospel in purity and peace; and whereas in our settling (by a wise providence of God) we are further dispersed upon the sea coasts and rivers than was at first intended, …" These earliest of colonists were not just looking for freedom and fortune but were also dedicated to advancing Christianity in a new country, America.

These people coveted religious freedom, and in their perilous journeys they brought with them Christian ideals and beliefs. Their leaders were Anglicans who set up the first churches in the new land. Knowing this about our earliest colonists, can we have any doubt that America's founding had significant Christian influence?

As more Englishmen came to America, the Anglican Church, the Church of England, began to grow and became the dominant church for the colonists along the coastal regions. Its influence eventually became diluted by an influx of reformed Christian denominations seeking religious liberty, such as the Puritans, Baptists, Dutch Reformed, and Congregationalists.

Inland from the Anglican Atlantic coast, the Appalachian frontier was dominated by Scotch-Irish migrating from their northeastern ports of entry down the Appalachian and Allegheny mountain chains and bringing different views of the Christian religion. As the call for independence became louder and the revolution got underway, many Anglicans who tended to be loyalists to the Crown, including the clergy, packed their bags and went back to England. The reformed churches filled the void, and it was they who became the leaders who made the American religious history that we know. To be sure, many of the Founders were members of the Anglican Church, but having lived under the tyranny of the English Crown, they recognized the need for religious freedom. It was many of them who, echoing the words of the Declaration, with a firm reliance on the protection of divine Providence, mutually pledged to each other their lives, their fortunes and their sacred honor. Without them you would not be here today.

Not long after the American Revolution, in 1787, *The Northwest Ordinance* establishing the Midwestern territories out to the Mississippi River had this to say about religion in Article 3: "Religion, morality, and knowledge, being necessary to good government and the happiness of mankind, schools and the means of education shall forever be encouraged." One can be sure that the authors of the Ordinance had Christianity in mind when they used the term "religion," the basis for their new settlements.

Mighty historical events seem to have converged in the sixteenth and seventeenth centuries to form the basis of what America is. It is as though there was "such a great cloud of witnesses" (Heb 12:11) who went before us, just as there was before the writer of Hebrews and the Apostolic Fathers. Although recognition of America's Christian roots are all but forgotten today, a great reliance upon God was evident during the founding of the nation. Even as the states were formed, God was mentioned in every state constitution, save one. This reflected a time when people depended on God for their work and gave thanks for His grace to them.[6]

In summary, this is how the Christian religion became so embedded in early America, a nation founded on the Christian principles its immigrants brought with them. It was settled and led by Christian people who knew their Creator and Savior. They built churches and allowed their lives to be driven by God's laws, thus forming the basis of a great nation. If there had been no Christian faith to provide the root system for the young country, there would have been no America with the fundamental principles of freedom and justice we have today.

What Did the Founders Say About Christianity?

The Founders had plenty to say about their faith and the role of religion in government and society. Their comments are too numerous to list here in great detail, but these few quotes should serve to illustrate the high priority our greatest leaders gave to Christian principles in the new nation:

- **George Washington (1732-1799)** was a member of the Continental Congress; Commander-in-Chief of the Continental Army; president of the Constitutional Convention; first President of the United States; "father of his country":

   "You do well to wish to learn our arts and ways of life, and above all, the religion of Jesus Christ. These will make you a greater and happier people than you are."

- **John Adams (1735-1826)** was a signer of the Declaration of Independence; judge; diplomat; Second President of the United States:

---

[6] Readers interested in having a deeper understanding of the influence of Christianity on America are encouraged to take advantage of the resources available from Wallbuilders. com, a premier repository and expositor on the faith of the Founding Fathers.

"The general principles on which the fathers achieved independence were the general principles of Christianity. I will avow that I then believed, and now believe, that those general principles of Christianity are as eternal and immutable as the existence and attributes of God."

"Without religion, this world would be something not fit to be mentioned in polite company: I mean hell."

"The Christian religion is, above all the religions that ever prevailed or existed in ancient or modern times, the religion of wisdom, virtue, equity and humanity."

+ **Benjamin Rush (1746-1813)** was a signer of the Declaration of Independence; surgeon general of the Continental Army; ratifier of the U. S. Constitution; "father of American medicine"; Treasurer of the U. S. Mint; "Father of public schools under the Constitution":

    "The Gospel of Jesus Christ prescribes the wisest rules for just conduct in every situation of life. Happy they who are enabled to obey them in all situations! ... My only hope of salvation is in the infinite transcendent love of God manifested to the world by the death of His Son upon the Cross. Nothing but His blood will wash away my sins [Acts 22:16]. I rely exclusively upon it. Come, Lord Jesus! Come quickly!" [Revelation 22:20].

+ **James Madison (1751-1836)** was a signer of the Constitution; author of the Federalist Papers; framer of the Bill of Rights; Secretary of State; fourth President of the United States:

    "I have sometimes thought there could not be a stronger testimony in favor of religion or against temporal enjoyments, even the most rational and manly, than for men who occupy the most honorable and gainful departments and [who] are rising in reputation and wealth, publicly to declare their

> *unsatisfactoriness by becoming fervent advocates in the cause of Christ; and I wish you may give in your evidence in this way."*

There is a criticism often directed at the Founders that tries to minimize their Christianity by labeling them as "deists." A deist believes that a creator God does exist, but that after the motions of the universe were set in place He retreated, having no further interaction with the created universe or the beings within it. When one examines the Christian statements by the Founders, one sees that few were deists by this definition. Consider also that all 56 signers of the Declaration of Independence were affiliated with a Christian church, and 24 had seminary or Bible school degrees. Thirty seven of the 55 signers of the United States Constitution were Christians. This does not look like a group of deists.

What About the "Unchristian" Side of American History?

In spite of the positive influence of the Christian faith on America, there are distinct, undeniable blemishes on our history, the results of which we live with to this day: the voyages of Columbus and other Spanish expeditions that, despite their Christian missionary goals, often brought harm to the native peoples they encountered. Another is the institution of slavery in both the South and the North and segregation in the post-Civil War South. Yet another is the treatment of the American Indians, who endured violence, dislocation, and internment on reservations. These issues must be addressed to maintain truthfulness and credibility in our view of history. However, it is important to remember that these blemishes on America were *not* the fault of Christianity but of flawed Christians. Yes, much of the history for which we credit the faith that was brought to the New World is also fraught with actions carried out by people, sometimes in the name of God, who were not ideal Christians. But you should not let people dismiss the role of Christianity in American history or characterize the United States as a force for evil in the world because of the actions and policies of some Americans who call themselves Christian.

There is a lesson here. Christian people are sinners like everyone else, and like everyone else they can act in a sinful way just as the Apostle Paul told us: "The acts of the sinful nature are obvious: sexual immorality, impurity and debauchery; idolatry and witchcraft; hatred, discord, jealousy, fits of rage, selfish ambition, dissensions, factions and envy; drunkenness, orgies, and the like. I warn you, as I did before, that those who live like this will not inherit the kingdom of God" (Galatians 5:19-21).

Such behavior comes when we practice our religion legalistically, not as a personal faith and guided by Scripture. It is not lived. When we live our faith independent of the formal religion but based on a personal relationship with God through His Son Jesus, who was sent for that very purpose, then we are open to His Holy Spirit to guide our conscience. Rather than acts of the flesh, our acts become fruit of the Spirit, which is quite different: "But the fruit of the Spirit is love, joy, peace, forbearance, kindness, goodness, faithfulness, gentleness and self-control. Against such things there is no law" (Galatians 5:22-23).

America still remains the exception among nations when it comes to freedom, opportunity, and the importance of the individual, regardless of race or creed. America's history has been a continuing story of doing good, standing up against evil and oppressive regimes, and aiding underdeveloped nations and those who have suffered catastrophes. In short, America is a leader among nations and has been viewed that way for a long time.

Many revisionist historians have attempted to distort American history to accommodate their own political aims and agendas. Others have, perhaps unintentionally, merely repeated the biased views that they were taught. Do not accept the skeptic's view that there is no God and that America's settlers were not really following Him. Do not let leftist historians and politicians tell you that America has not been a force for good in the world. When it comes to history, just as with Scripture, it is always best to go to the original sources of information. See what the Founders said in their own words, visit the monuments and edifices that honor them, and consider the eternal values on which they based their new nation. Only when we do this can we fully understand their intent as believing Christians.

There are many people and nations who would like to conquer or do away with America. They understand that to destroy America, they must do it from within, as Abraham Lincoln suggested: "All the armies of Europe, Asia and Africa combined, with all the treasure of the earth (our own excepted) in their military chest, with a Bonaparte for a commander, could not by force, take a drink from the Ohio, or make a track on the Blue Ridge in a trial of a thousand years. At what point then is the approach of danger to be expected? I answer, if it ever reach us, it must spring up amongst us. It cannot come from abroad. If destruction be our lot, we must ourselves be its author and finisher. As a nation of freemen, we must live through all time, or die by suicide" (January 27, 1838).

Because it was the Christian faith that was most responsible for America, the key to destroying America from within lies in removing or diluting that faith as a positive influence on the affairs of Americans and their government. That process has begun; it must be resisted by determined, well-informed, believers. Will you be one of them?

PART II

The Convergence of Biblical and Scientific Truth

CHAPTER 5

What Is Science?

On graduating from high school and preparing for your next phase of life, you are, it is probably safe to say, in some state of confusion about the relationship of the Bible and science. You are not alone. Neither the church nor the science classroom has done much to clarify what constitutes truth in this arena. We all have sat through those science classes and heard how long it took for plants and animals to evolve from lower forms to higher forms, and then we go to church and hear that every day for six days God created something new, beginning with the heavens and the earth.

Both views claim they have the truth, and too often you hear that, if you do not accept their view, something is either wrong with you spiritually or you are intellectually deficient. So what is the truth? Can science be true as well as the Genesis account? If you do not know some facts, it can be intellectually confusing. Both the church and the classroom are in error for taking extreme views that exclude a total consideration of the data available. There can be only one truth about any matter, but if both sides are claiming the exclusive truth, then one is wrong. Alternatively, both can be right if the correct understanding of the issue shows that they both agree.

This chapter begins with the premise that the Bible is true because it is God's Word. It also assumes that science is true. In regard to creation and the origin of man, they now come closer together. We attempt here to present factual information with the expectation that you will use your God-given intellectual ability to arrive at the truth. First, let's understand what science is all about.

G. Lee Southard, Ph.D.

What Is the Definition of Science?

Science is the search for truth. Scientific experimentation measures things, collects data and applies mathematics. Collection of enough data through repetitive experiments usually results in conclusions leading to hypotheses, theories, and subsequently scientific truth.

Through the collection of data, science is constantly peeling back the mystery of how the universe, the earth, and life on earth were created and continue to exist. As a result of scientific data and observation, theories have emerged to explain these creations. In the creation of the universe and earth it is called the Big Bang Theory (BBT); for the creation of the earth we have the geological time scale (GTS) and the fossil record; and for the creation of living things we have the fossil record, the theory of evolution (TOE), and now the genetic code. If we go back in time on any of these, they all have in common a beginning and and a continuing flow of scientific discovery yielding information that increases our understanding. Many of these new scientific understandings point to an intelligent design (ID).

What Is Intelligent Design?

Intelligent design is a scientific theory because it uses the four-step process of the scientific method. These steps involve observation, hypothesis, experiment, and a conclusion. Intelligent design begins with the observation that complex specified information (CSI) is produced by intelligent agent(s). Design theorists hypothesize that if a natural object was designed, it will contain high levels of CSI. Scientists then perform experimental tests upon natural objects to determine if they contain complex and specified information. A testable form of CSI is irreducible complexity, which can be discovered by experimentally reverse-engineering biological structures to see if they require all of their parts to function. When ID researchers find irreducible complexity in biology, they conclude that such structures were designed.

An example of where intelligent design can be found is in the Big Bang Theory. The BBT states that the creation of space, time and matter came from a single point of infinite energy. That point of infinite energy was the beginning, and a beginning suggests a beginner. Scientific data from astronomy, physics, mathematics, geology and chemistry produced the BBT that describes an exquisite creation from a beginning before which there was no matter, space, or time. A beginning requires something or someone to begin it. So what or who is behind the point of beginning? Some speak of a force or a designer. Some flat out call the beginner God, the creator. Many scientists will not accept ID because they feel the term ID masquerades as a cover for God and a form of creationism. For some scientists, to invoke God as a causative agent is to invoke the supernatural, which by definition is not measureable.

Another example where ID can be found is in the theory of evolution. The TOE states that there are changes in the heritable traits of biological populations over successive generations leading to new life forms. Heritable traits are passed from one generation to the next via DNA, a molecule that encodes genetic information, and a host of accompanying genetic processes. This has been taking place going back to an initial ancestral life form from which all life sprang. The point of a first life form would be a beginning, and this is where the TOE has no reasonable explanation. Who or what created the first life form, and how? It certainly was a very complicated process and very unlikely to arrive by pure chance. An intelligent designer is suggested because of the many complex and specified processes supporting life that appear to be information based.

Scientific data from the fields of paleontology, chemistry and biology lead to the existence of living species over millions if not billions of years. All of these living organisms have cellular processes that are very complex but function and maintain life exquisitely. In many cases these complex functions seem to operate off of some built-in intelligence, and in some cases they operate as if they have been programmed like a computer, for example the DNA code for protein synthesis.

Taking this line of thinking all the way back, this complexity had to be inherent in the very first life form. It is reasonable to ask, "Who or what caused the implantation of the first DNA in the first life form and what or who told it how to code?" To the naturalist and Darwinian evolutionist, this is known as the DNA enigma. Again, this speaks of an intelligent designer, and Christians will call the designer God. Some scientists will say this all came about by chance, but statisticians have calculated that to be impossible. The probability estimate for attaining the necessary characteristics for a life-supporting body such as earth is less than 1 chance in 10^{282} (million trillion) that even one such life-support body would occur anywhere in the universe without invoking divine miracles (Ross, April 2, 2004).

Not all scientists will agree that the observations point to a designer such as God. Rather, they attribute the observations to a cause currently beyond the reach of science or in science that has not yet been discovered. To many scientists, God as a designer does not fit into scientific thought because His realm is not measurable—it is considered supernatural. However, that does not mean that the understandings of our world derived from scientific experimentation and observation exclude the existence of a designer or the supernatural. In fact, the observations of science often point to phenomena of such exquisiteness and precision that a design is often invoked as an explanation. For scientists to reject the role of a designer in complex processes that have no scientific explanation is not scientific. If the data leads one to a hypothesis that there could be some other cause not explainable by science, then such an hypothesis needs to be considered, even if supernatural.

A Christian friend of mine in Colorado had a saying for things that just seemed right but had no objective evidence, nor could they be measured. Her saying was, "You know in your knower" that something is so. This is something we have probably all experienced. Another term for it is intuition, the ability to understand something immediately, without the need for conscious reasoning. While writing this book, I encountered a new book written by Douglas Axe, *Undeniable*, which deals with this very subject as it applies to intelligent design. It asserts that intuition is something developed in childhood and is scientifically valid, although it sometimes seems supernatural.

What Is the Supernatural?

The Oxford English Dictionary defines the supernatural as a manifestation or event attributed to some force beyond scientific understanding or the laws of nature. As such it is unmeasurable, and because of this science will not accept anything supernatural as a causative agent. **It can be argued that the supernatural is not part of science, but if science is the search for truth, then all possible truths including the supernatural must be considered if data points to it.**

Science also includes searching in the direction that the data points until the next set of data either confirms the direction or suggests a different one. It is possible that scientific inquiry may never lead to a supernatural truth, because the science could proceed along a single, fruitless path of inquiry for a very long time. That would not mean that a supernatural explanation is not there, only that it has not been measured.

To deny a supernatural explanation as a possible explanation for an observation is to deny the student the opportunity to apply reason to consider it. To deny supernatural consideration as a possibility for explanation because it is not measurable and might imply God, is to establish science as a God. So why don't boards of education in our school districts authorize the teaching of science in such a way that allows the student to consider intellectually that intelligent design or supernatural causes might be considered as possible causes?

What Is Scientific Naturalism?

We can speak of two different forms of scientific naturalism.

Methodological naturalism is the assumption that observable events in nature are explained by natural causes, without assuming the existence or non-existence of the supernatural. In other words, a supernatural explanation is acceptable only *if* the scientific data points to it. This is like Alvin Plantinga's definition of science that advocates letting the results from the search for truth take one to wherever it goes, without restriction. If the results do not lead to a scientific explanation and infer that a supernatural explanation could be possible, then a supernatural possibility has to be considered. Even Charles Darwin recognized that the Creator Himself might be involved in natural selection: "There is grandeur in this view of life with its several powers, having been originally breathed by the Creator into a few forms or into one; and that, whilst this planet has gone cycling on according to the law of gravity, from so simple a beginning endless forms most beautiful have been, and are being, evolved" (249).

73

Metaphysical naturalism is the assumption that nature is all there is. Everything has a scientific explanation, whether the explanation has been discovered or not. Supernatural explanations do not exist and therefore cannot be considered. Scientists who practice according to this view usually have a strong atheist bias, and there is a high degree of adamancy among such people.

Science students are taught to search for truth by pursuing natural causes and to continue until a natural explanation is found. The methodological naturalist will consider all the data and then follow where it leads. The metaphysical naturalist, however, will do the same but will not follow the possibility of a supernatural explanation. Metaphysical naturalism is what many college professors and high school teachers are teaching their students. As a result, the possibility of intelligent design or any other supernatural explanation is omitted, thus robbing the student of a chance to reason through a variety of possible explanations.

Is There a Conflict Between Science and the Bible?

> **"It is important to note that there can be no real conflict between the facts of the Bible and the facts of science, since God was the Author of both. The problems arise when we begin to interpret those facts" (BGEA, 6/1/2004).**

As a scientifically trained person and also a Christian, I understand this potential conflict because I have experienced it. However, as a Christian I believe that the God who created everything would have created the universe, earth, and life using processes that sometimes employ other processes, which we are now just beginning to understand. Stated another way, the more we learn and uncover through science, the more we realize what is unknown and how exquisite and precise is that which is known. Because God created man in His own image with intelligence, innate curiosity, and the ability to reason, man has been discovering how these marvelous processes work, and he will continue to do so in the future. If you choose to believe it, the scientific knowledge coming from such discoveries will continue to reveal the greatness and intelligence of God, who applied himself to exquisitely and precisely create man and an environment to support him for His own purpose, which is described in the Bible (Ephesians 1:2-12).

It is time to call a truce between those advocating the Bible over science and those advocating science over the Bible. The attacks have often been vicious and unkind and only serve to keep us away from the truth. Remember, the same God who gave us the Bible also gave us science. In the Bible He tells us what he did, and in through science we are allowed to determine how He did it.

The Bible says, "You shall know the truth and the truth will set you free." As Christians we think of the Bible as the Word of a sovereign God. Therefore, if God's Word is true then the Bible is the truth. For example, when in Genesis 1:1 it says **"In the beginning God created the heavens and the earth"** and goes on to describe a six-day creation culminating with man, believers in the Bible hold this to be true. However, not all Christians believe that the creation was done in six 24-hour days—some think that it happened over billions of years. Nevertheless, these young-earth and old-earth creationists can agree that God was the creator, which is at odds with non-creationists who attribute everything to evolution and natural processes. You may be surprised that many scientists believe that the creator is God.

Still, there can be only one truth. Scientific inquiry and the Bible should arrive at the same truth! An examination of the two indicates that they do, but certain extremists of scientific opinion on the one hand and religious opinion on the other hand maintain that science and the Bible are not compatible. These extremists do a great injustice, particularly to young people who seek a better understanding of the truth.

Christians and scientists equally share the blame for placing science and the Bible in conflict. Christians see God as the creator and intervener behind creation and the development of life, but not by chance or natural selection (evolution) as science sees creation. Christians see scientists as having an agenda that disregards the existence of God and pushes evolution in direct opposition to the creation account found in Genesis. Some Christians think all scientists are atheists. Some scientists see Christians as dogmatic and unaccepting of the results of scientific inquiry. Some scientists do not accept the intervention of God as an explanation because it is supernatural and cannot be experimentally tested. Scientists see Christians as entrenched in certain biblical beliefs to the point where, if a scientific explanation agrees with the belief, it will not be accepted simply because it is science.

It is a goal of this chapter to arrive at a point where the truth of the Bible is supported by the results of scientific inquiry and thus they are in agreement. For the biblical reader who begins with a fundamental assumption that the Bible is true, this might require an alternative interpretation of Scripture that may vary from a traditional interpretation but still be in accordance with what the Bible says in its original language. For the scientist this will require an extrapolation of data that is currently unexplainable by science but still points to an intelligence as a causative agent. As has been discussed, creation, the origin of life, and many life-giving processes are examples of cases where an intelligent causative agent is a likely factor.

Creation of the universe, the earth, and the origin of man are of great interest to people of faith, atheists, and agnostics. Research scientists belong to all three categories, and over the past one hundred years the collective scientific understanding of creation and the origin of man has been exciting and enlightening. Nobel Prizes have been given for work in mathematics, physics, chemistry and biology. For those who are believers in God, this work has served to punctuate His majesty and glory.

Who Were the Great Scientists?

Many of the fathers of modern-day science and the church did not see science in conflict with the Bible. In fact, many scientists were Christians and claimed that discovering the ways of God was the foundation for their research. The Catholic Church encouraged education and scientific understanding, with the Jesuits making significant scientific contributions (cf. Woods 12/28/2011). Consider the following scientists:

+ **Nicholas Copernicus (1473-1543)** studied for the priesthood. In opposition to Catholic dogma at the time that the sun revolved around the earth, *geocentrism,* he mathematically proposed that the sun, not the Earth, was the center of the solar system. This is called the *heliocentric system.* This is the system we recognize as the modern ordering of the planets in our solar system. Copernicus said "My goal is to try to find the truth in God's majestic creation."

+ **Francis Bacon (1561-1627)** was a philosopher who is known for establishing the scientific method of inquiry based on experimentation and inductive reasoning. He rejected atheism as being the result of shallow philosophy. His goals were the discovery of truth, service to his country, and service to the church.

+ **Galileo Galilei (1564-1642)** was educated in a Jesuit monastery. He scientifically proved the Copernican theory, despite the church's order against it. He was persecuted for his work and ultimately jailed, not for the work but for lying. Galileo has been called the "father of modern observational astronomy," the "father of modern physics," and the "father of modern science." Galileo said, "God is known by nature in his divine works and by doctrine in His revealed word."

+ **Johannes Kepler (1571-1630)** was a sincere and pious Lutheran whose works on astronomy contain writings about how space and the heavenly bodies represent the Trinity. He was a brilliant mathematician and astronomer, did early work on light, and established the laws of planetary motion about the sun.

+ **Blaise Pascal (1623-1662)** was a French mathematician, physicist, inventor, writer, and theologian. He published a treatise on the subject of projective geometry and established the foundation for probability theory. He was raised a Roman Catholic and in 1654 had a vision of God, which redirected his study from science to theology, including a published work on the defense of Christianity. Pascal's last words were "May God never abandon me."

+ **Isaac Newton (1642-1720)** was considered by some to be the most influential scientist and mathematician of all time and was also the author of religious tracts. Scientifically he is remembered for the Newtonian laws of motion and universal gravitation. Newton said, "All created objects which represent order and life in the universe could happen only by the willing reasoning of its original creator whom I call the Lord God."

+ **Robert Boyle (1791-1867)** was the father of "Boyle's Law" which applies to gases. He was a Protestant and promoted the Christian religion abroad, financing the publishing of the New Testament into Irish and Turkish. Boyle wrote against atheists in his day. He is considered one of the founders of modern chemistry.

+ **Michael Faraday (1791-1867)** was one of the greatest scientists. His work on electricity and magnetism revolutionized physics. He also had many discoveries in the field of chemistry. Computers and telephones are traceable to his discoveries. Faraday was a Christian member of the Sandemanians, an offshoot of the Presbyterians that rejected the concept of state churches. He is remembered as a man whose sense of God pervaded his work.

+ **Gregor Mendel (1822-1884)** was an Austrian monk who created the science of genetics known as Mendelian inheritance. Mendel established many of the laws of heredity, but the significance of his research was not recognized until 30 years after his death. He also published in the field of meteorology.

+ **William Thomson Kelvin (1824-1907)** helped to lay the foundations of modern physics, contributing to the first and second laws of thermodynamics. He was a committed Christian. Lord Kelvin is known for his calculation of "Absolute Zero" as 273.15 degrees.

+ **James Clerk Maxwell (1831-1879)** is best known for formulating the theory of electromagnetic radiation. The Maxwell equations form the basis for this field. He was a strong Christian and student of the Bible who put his beliefs and the Bible to intellectual tests. Maxwell reasoned and predicted that the rings around Jupiter were particles, something not proved until the 1980s with the Voyager space missions. According to the Encyclopedia Britannica, "Maxwell is regarded by most modern physicists as the scientist of the 19th century who had the greatest influence on 20th century physics."

+ **Max Planck (1858-1947)** is known for the origination of quantum theory, which won him the Nobel Prize in Physics in 1918, and for his contributions to theoretical physics. Max Planck said, "Religion and science demand for their foundation faith in God … God stands for the former in the beginning, and for the latter at the end of the whole thinking. For the former, God represents the basis, for the latter—the crown of any reasoning concerning the world-view" (cited by DarwinThenAndNow.com).

+ **Albert Einstein (1879-1955)** was one of the best-known names of the twentieth century. He was the father of the Theory of Relativity and the conversion of matter to energy ($E=mc^2$). He did not believe in a personal God but recognized that the universe must have been created. Einstein once remarked to a young physicist, "I want to know how God created this world. I am not interested in this or that phenomenon, in the spectrum of this or that element. I want to know His thoughts, the rest are details." A famous saying of his was "Science without religion is lame, religion without science is blind."

+ **George Lemaitre (1894-1966)** was a physicist, Roman Catholic priest, and the father of the Big Bang Theory on the creation of the universe. Lemaitre said, "Does the Church need Science? Certainly not. The Cross and the Gospel are enough. However, nothing that is human can be foreign to the Christian. How could the Church not be interested in the most noble of all strictly human occupations, namely the search for truth?"

+ **Wernher von Braun (1912-1977)** developed the rockets that launched America's first space satellite and the first series of moon missions that included the Saturn V. Von Braun said, "My experiences with science led me to God. They challenge science to prove the existence of God. But must we really light a candle to see the sun?"

+ **Francis Collins (1950-)** is an American physician and geneticist noted for his research in genetics and ultimately leadership of the Human Genome Project. He is currently director of the National Institutes of Health (NIH) and author of the book *The Language of God: A Scientist Presents Evidence for Belief*. Collins believes that Christianity can be reconciled with evolution and science.

+ **Gerald Schroeder (ca. 1938-)** has a Ph.D. in nuclear physics and earth and planetary sciences from MIT and currently teaches at Aish Ha Torah College of Jewish Studies in Israel. He focuses on the relationship between science and spirituality. "Wisdom, information, an idea, is the link between the metaphysical Creator and the physical creation. It is the hidden face of God" (184).

In summary, God brought into being space, time and matter and provided a palate of information hidden behind them all. Because we are created in His image with intelligence and reasoning He allows us to seek and understand how He did it. We call it science. Because he had a supernatural purpose for the creation He provided a written story of why He did it and how He accomplished His intent, often using as His instrument His creation, man. We call that account the Holy Bible. It is time we see both science and the Bible as His story.

CHAPTER 6

What Is Evolution?

The Theory of Evolution is the ever present "elephant in the room" lurking in the background in any discussion involving science and the Bible, especially in reference to the origin of man. It is always in the background. Just the word "evolution" sparks anxiety, distrust, and defense mechanisms among Christians and between Christians and non-Christians. Evolution has taken on worldview proportions, and in so doing has become more adamantly against the role of God in creation of the universe, earth, and man. In this chapter we will attempt to see how evolution, the available science, and the Bible currently interface. This will be in preparation for addressing in the following chapters how science and the Bible compare regarding the creation of the universe, the earth, and the origin of man.

Evolution is defined as change over time, but when applied to life systems it means genetic changes in the populations of organisms over successive generations. In evolution many changes are the result of pure chance. Furthermore, evolution is a theory. When scientists define something as a theory, it means it is well understood, has been tested, and provides testable predictions. For evolution, this criterion holds less and less true as new data emerges. When Darwin first proposed the theory, it was based on paleontological and geological observations; none of today's science was known to him. Newer scientific findings in the areas of chemistry, biochemistry, biology, and physics point to explanations that are far beyond anything Darwin could have imagined.

One of the biggest complaints from Christians is the teaching of evolution in the high school or college classroom as indisputable fact. It is often dogmatic in its approach and excludes any scientific data that leads to alternative explanations such as intelligent design (ID) or any supernatural involvement. This practice denies one of the basic tenets of science, namely, that the search for scientific truth should proceed in the direction of where the data leads. The reason for this is that those in authority are more interested in fostering an agenda with an evolutionary worldview than in following the scientific evidence. They fear that, because ID can be used to infer an intelligent designer, Christians will call that designer God.

Evolution should not be confused with naturalism. Evolution is more of a process, while naturalism is more of a belief that only natural and not supernatural forces are at work in the world. Naturalism acknowledges no such person as God, nor anything like God; it contends that humans are strictly material objects with no soul or spirit (Plantinga, *Knowledge*, 8). Evolution is change over time regarding living things, where change is based on natural selection due to species adaptation for the purpose of survival and reproduction. Evolution does not by the strictest definition preclude God, for example microevolution. However, evolution is attractive to some with a world view counter to a belief in God as creator.

As discussed under the heading "What Is Intelligent Design?" there have been numerous scientific findings that now point to intelligent design in the way living things operate, even down to the molecular level. This brings up the question of whether intelligent design could include evolutionary processes. That is, could God have used evolution as a process to achieve his purposes by employing natural selection? To those seeking to include God in the evolutionary explanation, this is called Theistic Evolution, which we will talk more about in Chapter 8.

Evolution as a strictly natural process comes up short in having an explanation for certain questions, such as "How did life first form?" Because we now know that life in any form is dependent on a coded genetic program, the basic evolutionary concept of chance is very unlikely.

Evolution study is too large and complex to go into detail such as that found in a biology class. Our study here is an overview and supplemental to existing classroom courses; it focuses on evolution's weaknesses and areas of science that suggest explanations other than those of evolution. You are encouraged to go deeper in your investigation and studies by sifting and weighing what you hear and learn in the classroom. In your studies, consider that God is at work in science as well. Find Him in the classroom. What you know about the theory of evolution and how you perceive it will help you be a more effective ambassador for Christ (cf. Rana, *Through the Lens*).

What Are The Categories of Evolution?

Evolution is divided into five categories. Microevolution, speciation, and microbial evolution are acceptable to Christians, while macroevolution and chemical evolution are not. As we will see later, science appears to be on the side of the Christian view.

> Microevolution – there is evidence for it—acceptable to Christians;
> Speciation - there is evidence for it—acceptable to Christians;
> Microbial Evolution - there is evidence for it—acceptable to Christians;
> Chemical Evolution – it is scientifically challenged—unacceptable to Christians;
> Macroevolution – it is scientifically challenged—unacceptable to Christians.

Microevolution refers to variation within a single species, not the creation of a new species. Microevolution changes may occur either as a result of environmental changes, where the species adapts, or as the result of genetic drift, which occurs when a variant form of a gene, called an allele, increases or decreases by chance over time, usually in small populations. Either way, the species adapts. An example is the sparrow. The sparrow in the north is larger-bodied to withstand cold weather, where the southern sparrow is slimmer. Insects developing resistance to the application of pesticides is another example of microevolution.

Speciation refers to microevolution over a long period, but is not capable of producing a new species. Speciation occurs when one population of species gets isolated from another population and a difference develops, producing a sister species, for example, domestic cattle, the ox, and the yak.

Microbial evolution happens among viruses, bacteria, and single-celled organisms, but it does not produce a new species. An example is the development of resistance of bacteria due to antibiotic use over time. Antibiotics do not kill all bacteria, but through the effect on the organism's metabolism some survive. Survivors then modify their response to the antibiotic and become more resistant the next time they encounter the same antibiotic. Penicillin and the tetracyclines are examples of antibiotics to which resistance has developed. Antimicrobial agents such as ethyl alcohol, iodine, and chlorhexidine are examples of products that kill bacteria, leaving no survivors and therefore no resistance.

Chemical evolution, also known as abiogenesis, explains the origin of life happening through random chemical reactions that produce the materials necessary to create life. This is sometimes referred to as having taken place in the primordial soup millions of years ago. Scientists have considered this possibility and determined that the probability of producing life by chance by abiogenesis is nil; it is impossible. Scientists in the past have attempted to mimic this process through laboratory experiments using conditions they believed existed when life would have first begun. The Miller-Urey experiments of the 1950s tested the theory that amino acids (the building blocks of life) were formed by chance over several billions of years from when water appeared on earth. Miller and Urey mixed what were thought to be the likely chemical precursors (water, ammonia, and methane) and simulated environmental conditions (an electric spark) present on earth at that time. The experiment demonstrated that amino acids could indeed be created.

The experimental results were interesting, but it was later determined that the atmosphere on the reactants was not that of the early earth when such an event would have taken place. In addition, the steps to life would have involved much more than the synthesis of a group of random amino acids. The amino acids required for life would have needed to be just the right 21, in just the right stereochemistry, and having available just the right proteins, DNA, and RNA. There was also a host of additional biological and chemical triggers of just the right type that needed to be synthesized to produce a protein. This is why the probability of chemical evolution is so low. Something a lot less random would be required.

Macroevolution is thought of as the transformation of one major biological group into another biological group of entirely new creatures. However, it goes deeper than that. Macroevolution also encompasses universal common descent, the idea that every living organism descended from a universal common ancestor (UCA; or LUCA, last universal common ancestor). Not everyone agrees that this is possible, even among evolutionary biologists. Advocates would cite as examples dinosaurs evolving into birds, wolf-like creatures evolving into whales, and apes evolving into human beings.[7] In addition, there is a tendency to say that, because microevolution is true and verifiable, macroevolution must also be true. However, indisputable data for macroevolution does not exist. The reason it does not exist is due to lack of provable transitional forms in the fossil record. This is because the fossil record is incomplete—it is not possible to establish a point of divergence of one species into another. Those scientists who have attempted to do so are actually making an assumption that a so-called transitional fossil is an ancestor of a more recent one. When it comes to macroevolution, there are significant factors that have emerged from the study of evolution that cast doubt on it.

What Are Some Things That Question Evolution?

What Is Convergent Evolution?

Convergent evolution (CE) is a term that has been used to describe the independent presence of similar features in different species that are not closely related and not through common descent. Convergent evolution creates analogous structures that have similar form or function, but these features were not present in the last common ancestor of those groups (Reece, 472). Two examples of CE are bats and insects; while they both have wings and can fly, their wings were not inherited from a common ancestor, but the forelimbs that serve as wings were inherited.

There are many organs in different animals that are similar, the most interesting being the eye. The eye is similar in vertebrates and in mollusks, e.g., humans and octopi, animals of completely different phyla. It has been found that the same gene in all phyla is responsible for the formation of the eye. The eye-responsible gene has even been found in eyeless animal forms that predate the animal forms with eyes. This would argue for the occurrence of a genetic mutation that would cause the gene in an eyeless animal to develop eyes. The evolutionist would claim this to be a random mutation. However, the statistical probability of a random mutation is impossible.

---

[7] For more information on UCA, the reader is referred to the discussion by Douglas L. Theobold, "29+Evidences."

Gerald Schroeder says that the "Convergent traits among animals of different phyla have challenged the very basis of evolutionary theory: the hypothesis that traits develop independently, initiated at the molecular level by random-point mutations" (118). Schroeder goes on to state that convergent evolution appears to have been preprogrammed. Programming requires a programmer, which is another example of intelligent design.

What Was the Cambrian Explosion?

The Cambrian Explosion was the sudden appearance in the fossil record of major animal forms about 540 million years ago. Fossils show that most living organisms prior to the explosion were simple and multicellular. The Cambrian fossils were more complex. The fossils associated with the Cambrian (formerly called Silurian) explosion of life were found in 1886 in the Canadian Rockies in what is known as the Burgess Shale Area. The Burgess Shale Area was once part of the Pacific Ocean, but over time it had been exposed by retreating seas and upheavals in the landmass to form the mountains. The Cambrian explosion consisted of about 70 different complex animal phyla (groups of animals with the same body layout). These soft tissue animals had been sealed and preserved.

Over the approximately 20 million years of the Cambrian explosion **there is no evidence of any evolutionary process having taken place**, and the basic anatomy of every animal alive today was present during the Cambrian Period. The fossils uncovered were relatives of crustaceans and starfish, sponges, mollusks, worms, chordates, and algae. About 30 of the phyla discovered are still present today.

A second explosion of life called the Avalon explosion is proposed to have occurred about 33 million years earlier. There is little known about it except that it was in the form of multicellular macroscopic life forms unrelated to the Cambrian animals, and they disappeared with the Cambrian.

When he published *On the Origin of the Species* in 1859, Darwin knew that fossils existed from the Silurian Explosion. He also knew that these findings would be problematic for his theory because evolutionary processes should occur at a slow pace, not appear suddenly (Darwin, 313-314). A slow pace should have produced transitional life forms for the animals found in the Cambrian layer, but there are none. Evolutionists dispute this reasoning, stating that the time period for their appearance might not be a problem due to the simplicity of the life forms and the possible change in environmental factors favorable to life. In any case, transitional life forms are essential for macroevolution to be true, and the Cambrian fossils have none over the 20 million years. Creationists, on the other hand, believe that in the absence of transitional life forms the Cambrian explosion is evidence for a supernatural intervention on a mass scale.

Before citing the Cambrian explosion is labeled as a supernatural event, which it might be, young earth creationist need to remember that the event is well dated and did not occur in a single day.

What Are Transitional Life Forms?

According to the macroevolution model, where one major ancestral biological group is transformed into a new major descendant biological group, we would expect to see a trail of intermediate species numbering in the millions and including at least an equal number of failed species for every successful one. Intermediate species would reflect gradual changes in morphology that would show the evolution of one group to another in distinct stages. These intermediate species are known as transitional life forms. Darwin noted the lack of transitional fossils at the time of his writing, but he expected that more discoveries would fill in the gaps. However, if such forms fail to materialize, it would constitute an objection to his theory.

Transitional forms are expected to represent changes in morphology and anatomy, such as feathered wings for birds or appendages for water animals to migrate onto land, but the transition does not make them ancestors. For example, *Archaeopteryx*, having a dinosaur-like body and feathered wings appears to be a transitional form between the dinosaurs and birds. However, it is not the most recent common ancestor of all birds and it is not a direct ancestor of any species of bird alive today.

Human evolution can be declared a fact only when the necessary transitional forms can be found and linked together through progressive change. A group of ape-like life forms called hominids are considered by evolutionary biologists to be transitional forms for human evolution. However, the connection between any of them and humans remains problematic.

G. Lee Southard, Ph.D.

Does Probability Apply To Evolution?

Probability is a mathematical calculation used to determine if something is likely to occur. Numerous mathematical probability calculations have been applied to evolution, and to go into them here would be beyond the scope of this book. Evolutionists believe that even though the probability is low, given enough time things would have happened to produce human evolution. But evolution and its processes fail probability calculations at every stage. To demonstrate this, consider that the very simplest and first life form would have required the creation of the right chemicals, a protein, an amino acid, and the more complex DNA. This process is most elaborate, so don't tune out—instead, keep reading and let it impress on you how unlikely it is that life developed by chance.

First, there are many proteins needed for life. Second, amino acids are necessary to make up the protein, and there are 20 needed for life. Each of the amino acids needs to be made, and each has carbon, hydrogen, nitrogen, oxygen, and sometime sulfur. These elements need to be assembled in just the right way to make the amino acid. The amino acids, having asymmetric centers, have the ability to be in two stereochemical isomers called D and L forms. In the case of amino acids in life forms, only the L form is acceptable. Each amino acid must be transported to the DNA molecule Both the DNA and the transporting molecule must have also been synthesized prior to the transport. Once each amino acid has been transported to the DNA in just the right order so it can be inserted in the protein chain in just the right position to provide a properly functioning protein.

The DNA is made up of the elements of carbon, hydrogen, nitrogen, oxygen, and phosphorus assembled in a way to have made four nucleotides and phosphate groups, each by an entirely separate chemistry. Furthermore, the four nucleotides also have asymmetric centers, but now they must be in the D form. Then the DNA sequence of nucleotides and phosphates must be paired with another nucleotide to form a base pairing in just the right order to produce what is essentially a digital code, so that the protein could be assembled in just the right order of amino acids. If this sounds complicated, it is, but there is more.

The DNA must take the form of an alpha helix (think spiral staircase with first step on the left formed by hydrogen bonding between the nucleotides and spiraling to the right). Then the protein produced must fold up in a three-dimensional state that will allow it to fit into a receptor site to produce its effect, much like a key is made to fit into a lock to open or close a door. The likelihood of all this occurring by chance is impossible by probability standards. For a greater discussion with specific examples, I refer you to *The Science of God* by Gerald Schroeder. It advances theories about the reconciliation of faith and science, and in a discussion of the origin of life and evolution, it sees the statistical probabilities of such events as extremely improbable.

What Is the DNA Enigma?

The DNA enigma is an expression that defines this question: Where did the information come from that determines what protein to make in protein synthesis? DNA and protein data of samples taken from different living species suggests an evolutionary process because of the similarity of DNA and amino acid sequence data of protein among species. But it also presents a problem to evolution (Meyer, 223-224).

The function of DNA in every living cell is to manufacture proteins that are essential to life. The protein that is manufactured is dependent on the base pairing arrangement of four nucleotide bases that connect the two strands of DNA through hydrogen bonding. These four base pairs when put together become a code. The amino acids are brought to the DNA in the order in which the nucleotide base pairs need them, and the DNA according to its code manufactures the correct protein from the assembling of amino acids in the proper sequence. How then did the chemical synthesis being done know what protein to make?

In the cell, the protein synthesis and assemblage is being driven by information very much like a computer program drives information based on a digital code developed by a programmer. Where does the information come from that tells the DNA what to do, how to do it, and when to do it? Since digital codes for computers are developed by man by application of intelligence, it is natural to think that any biological process requiring information also requires an intelligence to function. Who put the information there? It was hugely improbable that it was done by chance. The

DNA enigma reaches its peak when one considers how all this happened to make the very first life form.

The enigma is not just confined to DNA. Consider the myriad of other cellular functions and processes that operate on a basis of information providing instruction for them to do what they do. How were these developed? Since these processes speak of a high level of precision and exquisiteness, the conclusion has to be one of intelligent design. An intelligent design suggests a designer, an intelligent one at that. At least 700 scientists, including this writer, have signed the statement issued by "Dissent From Darwin": "We are skeptical of claims for the ability of random mutations and natural selection to account for the complexity of life. Careful examination of the evidence for Darwinian theory should be encouraged."

What Is Irreducible Complexity?

Irreducible complexity is a term coined by Michael Behe to describe "a single system composed of several well-matched, interacting parts that contribute to the basic function, wherein the removal of any one of the parts causes the system to effectively cease functioning" (Behe, 39). Behe cites the common household mousetrap as an example. If one part is missing, it doesn't just function with less efficiency; it doesn't function at all.

Biologically there are many cellular processes that are irreducibly complex. Some examples would be (a) the mechanism of blood clotting that involves two systems and 10 steps (Thrombocyte.com, 2016), (b) the DNA synthesis of a protein described previously, (c) the functioning eye. None of these processes functioned until fully assembled with all its parts or steps. Each step is of complex and specific design.

What Is the Evolutionary Worldview?

In many respects, evolution has become a worldview. A worldview is a particular philosophy of life or conception of the world (OED). What you believe, and how these beliefs influence you regarding what goes on in the world, is a result of your worldview. The evolutionary worldview relies completely on scientific knowledge and reason to explain man's past, man's evolvement into the present, and man's future destiny through evolutionary process.

Evolution's worldview is captured by John Stewart, a member of the Evolution, Complexity and Cognition Research Group at The Free University of Brussels, in his *Evolutionary Manifesto*. The manifesto states that it "is an intentional attempt to promote the shift to conscious evolution and the evolutionary activism that will drive it." It seeks a global consciousness and the development of a global society. Part 2 of the manifesto has a position on religion, stating " …they [religions] have typically promoted surrender to 'the absolute,' acceptance of whatever happens in the world and even physical withdrawal from normal daily life. Their maxim has been 'Thy will be done' rather than 'My will be done.'" Stewart further argues that evolution and the continuing revelations of science provide humanity with the only way to live life with meaningfulness and purpose. His third paragraph begins with the words "At present humanity is lost," which brings us to one of the purposes of this book, namely to show that we are *not* lost.

In short, there is no place for God in the strict evolutionary worldview. Not all people who believe in evolution would subscribe to the *Evolutionary Manifesto*. They would believe in the fundamentals of evolution that creation of the heavens and the earth and all of life happened by chance as part of natural processes. They would also advocate that there was no supernatural being involved, but they would not share Stewart's activism.

The evolutionary worldview has a level of activism that reaches into the classroom. At the core of evolution activism is a demand that only evolution be taught in the classrooms of America. There is no place for any other view, particularly anything that might lead to the student invoking God.

One such activist group is the National Center for Science Education (NCSE) whose tag line is "Defending the Teaching of Evolution and Climate Science." One of their stated tenets is to supply needed information and advice to defend what they term "good science" education at local, state, and national levels. These tenets sound good at first glance, because who doesn't want good science? But what is good science to NCSE? It is not allowing alternative explanations for the findings of science that don't fit into the evolutionary dogma. As noted earlier, this is not science because it violates the very definition of science.

According to the NCSE, opposing views should not be allowed. I, however, believe that opposing views such as creationism and intelligent design should be allowed and the decisions left up to the students once they have all the facts. Let the students intellectually analyze competing views. Let the students reason it out and sift through alternative views and vigorously debate. Isn't that what we want our graduates to be, free thinkers and apply reason? Unfortunately, the evolutionary worldview often drives the agenda.

This raises the question of whether those in the scientific community who advocate Darwinism have forgotten the true meaning of the scientific approach to truth and have become authoritative in their dealings. Darwinism and evolution have enough weaknesses that alternative explanations should certainly be allowed.

Atheists (those who lack a belief in God) such as Richard Dawkins, Fellow of the Royal Society, the Royal Society of Literature and the Royal College at Oxford, capture the view of evolutionists in this statement: "Evolution is a fact. Beyond reasonable doubt, beyond serious doubt, beyond sane, informed, intelligent doubt, beyond doubt evolution is a fact ... That didn't have to be true. It is not self-evidently, tautologically, obviously true, and there was a time when most people, even educated people, thought it wasn't. It didn't have to be true, but it is ... Evolution is the only game in town, the greatest show on earth" (8-9).

Perhaps it is worth taking time to say something about atheism, since evolution appears to be one of the atheists' weapons to take up against Christianity. Richard Dawkins, cited above, is one of the leading atheists today, the others being Daniel Dennett and Sam Harris. Christopher Hitchens, now deceased, was one who was seen frequently on television. All of these men are very intelligent and articulate. However, what they say about Christianity and Christians is no more than just that, sayings. The sayings are not based on any facts or data; they are merely exclamations that you are not expected to question. While none of us can absolutely prove the existence of God, we also cannot disprove it. As we have shown in this book and in many other books by astute authors, there is more evidence leading *to* Him than leading *away* from him.

In summary, evolution as the complete explanation for how living organisms came into being over time has become more questionable; it serves to fuel the controversy that has surrounded evolution ever since Darwin first offered it. How questionable and how controversial it is depends on one's worldview. Evolution has served as a way to explain in a somewhat systematic and scientific way how the various species might have arisen and how they might relate to each other, but there are a lot of information gaps in the theory. New scientific findings increasingly point to intelligent design in explaining the origin of man, the pinnacle of all species and of God's creation, and in biological processes essential to maintaining life.

CHAPTER 7

What About Creation?

"If you cannot see God in all, you cannot see God at all."
Anonymous

Was the Creation Planned by God?

Several years ago my wife and I were returning to Fort Collins, Colorado from Saratoga, Wyoming by way of Snowy Range Pass. It was summer and about midnight. We stopped for a rest break at the peak of the pass, about 10,000 feet. It was as dark as a coal bin at midnight. When we looked up at the stars, we expected to see a dark night sky with a few stars. Instead we saw a white sky punctuated by a few patches of blackness. Being Christians we were struck by the greatness, power, and majesty of the creator God. We were looking at an expanding universe and we could feel the presence of its creator. We were awestruck. The light of the stars we were observing had sent their light to us millions of years ago.

Whether you see creation as just a matter of chance or as the work of an almighty creator, you pause in wonderment. This wonderment extends throughout earthly creation as well, when one sees the intricate and precise myriad of processes that operate 24/7 to sustain life. It seems that this wonderment has a purpose to it, and a purpose is usually preceded by a plan.

What Was Pre-Creation?

The Bible speaks about what we can call pre-creation. There is no science that supports pre-creation because it occurred before there was space, time,

95

and matter. Pre-creation belongs to the realm of the unmeasureable. It is difficult to fathom because we are used to relating everything to time and measurable events, but time did not exist until creation, nor did matter and space. Space, matter, and time came into being at creation. Pre-creation was a "time" before time, and God described it best when he said, "I AM." He was before time began, during time, and after time will cease to be. So what do we know about pre-creation?

The Bible speaks of pre-creation in several places, often in terms of "before the creation of the world." For example, in Proverbs 8:22 (NLT), "wisdom" is personified and speaks of being present before the creation: "The LORD formed me from the beginning, before he created anything else." Christ is also described as being present at the creation: "He was with God in the beginning" (John 1:2). So the Bible references a pre-creation.

A fundamental question is: "Why did God create?" That is, "What was the purpose of creation?" Science has no answer for these questions, but the Bible does, and it has cosmic implications.

Scripture says that before the creation of the heavens and the earth described in Genesis 1, God had a plan. The plan intended and predestined us to be holy and blameless in his sight by sending Jesus Christ. This is a mind-stretching statement that might require time to sink in. Understanding it should aid you, as it did me, in comprehending a reason for creation, and that reason will impact your life as it did mine.

God's predestined plan had a purpose, and it is described by Paul the Apostle in Ephesians 1:4-6: "For he [God] chose us in him before the creation of the world to be holy and blameless in his sight. In love he predestined us for adoption to sonship through Jesus Christ, in accordance with his pleasure and will—to the praise of his glorious grace, which he has freely given us in the One he loves."

This plan was spoken of elsewhere as well. 1 Corinthians 2:6-8 tells us, "We do, however, speak a message of wisdom among the mature, but not the wisdom of this age or of the rulers of this age, who are coming to nothing. No, we declare God's wisdom, a mystery that has been hidden and that God destined for our glory before time began. None of the rulers of this age understood it, for if they had, they would not have crucified the Lord of glory." The Bible is clear that God's wisdom is a mystery; it has been hidden but is part of His plan that He destined for our glory before time began. Understanding and accepting this, God's pre-creation plan, not only helps in understanding why there was a creation but also points to a creator with sovereign credentials.

This raises a question regarding sin. In God's eyes, to "make us holy and blameless in His sight" would be to make us free from sin. Therefore, God would have known before the creation of man that sin would enter the world. The very fact that Satan came to Eve means that evil was already in the world, but it was unrecognizable as sin because Adam and Eve had not yet eaten of "the tree of the knowledge of good and evil" (Genesis 2:9). Did God intend for Adam and Eve to introduce sin into the world? Did God plan that Adam and Eve would choose to forsake the ideal life of the Garden of Eden for a life in a world of people that forever more would wrestle with the problem of sin? If the answer is "Yes!" why would God do this? Why would God have made this plan of predestined salvation and implemented it through His creation? It was because of love for the whole world (cf. Ephesians 1:4-5 cited above, and John 3:16) and perhaps the entire universe.

So *how* would He do this through creation? The answer may lie in Ephesians 3:10: "**His intent was that now, through the church, the manifold wisdom of God should be made known to the rulers and authorities in the heavenly realms** according to his eternal purpose which he accomplished in Christ Jesus our Lord" (emphasis added). There is no mention in this passage of God's wisdom being made known to earthly kingdoms or rulers. The passage only speaks of heavenly rulers and authorities. It is almost as though God, the Great "I AM," is using earth to demonstrate to heavenly authorities exactly what Ephesians 1 says about being made holy and blameless. Furthermore, He is going to do it through the very same people that He will find holy and blameless, the Church. Since He has charged the church to make this known and we are the church, this places an awesome responsibility upon us as the church.

At the heart of the matter, " ...our struggle is not against flesh and blood, but against the rulers, against the authorities, against the powers of this world's darkness, and against the spiritual forces of evil in the heavenly realms" (Ephesians 6:12 BSB). This means that our struggle with sin, which keeps us from being holy and blameless, is actually against the sinful forces of this world and the universe. Sounds a lot like spiritual warfare, doesn't it?

In summary, God had a purpose in creating the heavens and the earth. The core of this purpose included a relative short time span where God's created people could live on a planet made just right to support humans so that He could execute His eternal, universal plan of salvation.

What Are the Ten Most Important Words Ever Written?

Creation was the first step in God's pre-creation plan of predestination. For this reason the words "In the beginning God created the heavens and the earth" (Genesis 1:1) are the ten most important words ever written. Without the creation, nothing else matters. These ten words, believed by billions, have taken on new support from an unexpected source—that source is science. This should not be unexpected, because science also was created by a sovereign God who made everything. An objective study of the creation of the universe using both the Bible and emerging scientific understanding helps us to understand better the greatness of God and why He alone is worthy of praise and adoration.

For years some, both within and outside of the church, have contended that the Bible is not compatible with science, and vice versa. In public education, science is taught with no mention of the possibility of the divine or creator not even a generic intelligent designer. Both the church and public education must recognize that it is science that brings them together. Neither the church nor public education has recognized their emerging compatibility. As a result, you the student have been left in an educational void.

In the last 100 years science has confirmed many teachings of the Bible and, in the view of many, supported a case for an intelligent designer. In physics, chemistry, biology, astrophysics, genetics, etc., processes have been discovered and understood to the point where scientific explanations are not sufficient for how or why things work. For example, science cannot tell us who or what was behind the beginning of the universe, known as the Big Bang. Science knows life on earth had a beginning, but it cannot tell us what was behind the first life form or how it was created. Science cannot tell us what the intelligence is behind processes that appear to operate on information imparted from outside. Believers in God believe that He was behind all intelligence-based processes. If the science leads there, why not teach that as a possibility?

Among Christians there are different schools of thought concerning the role of science in creation. Some say there is no place at all for science in explaining the creation process for fear that the biblical meaning will be bent to serve a scientific end. But suppose the biblical meaning can stay intact? The best example is in asking the question, "How old is the universe and the earth?" The answer will be one of two schools of thought. They are young-earth creationists or old-earth creationists. Old-earth creationists believe there is compelling scientific evidence for a 13.8-billion-year-old universe and a 4.6-billion-year-old-earth. The young-earth belief is based on the interpretation of Genesis chapter 1 as a sequence of creation activities that was literally done in six 24-hour days. The young-earth creationists believe that not to accept the six 24-hour day interpretation, in spite of the science to the contrary, is to jeopardize the truth of the entire Bible, because if the creation cannot be accepted literally, the entire Bible could be flawed. One of the objectives of this chapter is to reconcile science with the Bible concerning creation.

What About Time?

As noted above, when Genesis divides the creation events into six days, a point of conflict about time emerges between young-earth and old-earth believers. The young-earth creationists believe that God created the heavens (universe) and the earth on Day 1 and then proceeded to create the systems that support life on successive days. Finally, the animals were created on Days 5 and 6 and man on Day 6 as the crown of God's creation.

Old-earth creationists, on the other hand, cite scientific data from the fossil record and geology as supporting an earth age of nearly 4 billion years. A reading of the Genesis account allows for an intellectually honest old-earth scenario totally in agreement with the biblical text This, reading is supported by an alternative but legitimate interpretation of the original Hebrew. The Hebrew word *yom*, which describes time, is used in the creation story in Genesis and has been translated into English and then interpreted to mean a 24-hour "day." However, *yom* has more than one Hebrew meaning regarding time. Yom can also mean a longer period of time. An analogy we might use today could be, "back in the day of our Founding Fathers," where we mean the period of Colonial America. No other biblical Hebrew word other than *yom* carries the meaning of a long period of time.[8]

---

[8] Many discussions based on the use of the word *yom* throughout the Old Testament are aimed at supporting both views. I encourage you to "Google" the term "Hebrew word for day in Genesis" and review the various opinions.

The Bible contains other passages that tend to support *yom* as meaning a longer period of time, as opposed to a 24-hour day. Some biblical descriptions of events include processes, and a process takes time. For example, Genesis 1 describes the creation of plants and fruit for man to eat; we know that these take time to grow. In Genesis 2:15-17 God made a garden called Eden and placed man in the garden. Adam is told he may eat of every tree of the garden except one, the tree of the knowledge of good and evil. A tree does not grow in a 24-hour day; it takes much more time.

There is another reason to believe that *yom* could mean a long period of time. The Jewish calendar does not date from creation but from Adam, omitting the six days of creation. This suggests that the early Hebrews may have recognized that they could only precisely date back to a known time. For them it was when Adam left the Garden of Eden. The period prior to Adam may have been uncertain to them at the time the calendar was written. Remember, Moses did not create the Jewish calendar. It was not created until the second century before Christ and was based strictly on the Genesis genealogy by counting years.

Young-earth creationists view creation as a literal six-day 24 hour per day creation event. This is a view that has no scientific support.

Regardless of view whether a person is young-earth or old-earth is immaterial when it comes to faith in the Lord Jesus. Young and old-earth creationists will rest for eternity in the presence of the Lord. Jesus never promised eternal salvation based on one's interpretation of the Bible, but rather on a belief in Him (John 3:16).

What *does* make a difference, however, is the way one approaches non-Christians who have an intellectual problem with the six-day creation story. If one uses a science-based and biblically-consistent time line where *yom* represents a period of time the old-earth earth view could keep the conversation going so that the salvation story can be presented.

What Was the Big Bang?

The Big Bang Theory is the prevailing scientific cosmological model for the creation of the universe. It was first proposed in 1927 by Georges Lemaître, a Belgian priest, astronomer, and physicist. Lemaître also demonstrated that the universe continues to expand. The Bible tells us that God spoke creation into existence, and the Big Bang is not in conflict with a creator. Science places the creation moment at approximately 13.8 billion years ago. This age of the universe is not to be confused with the age of the earth, which is about 4.6 billion years old. The age of the earth is based on evidence from radiometric dating of meteorite material found on earth; it is consistent with the radiometric ages of the oldest-known terrestrial samples returned from the moon. The heavens we see on a dark night contain billions of galaxies in addition to our own galaxy, and they were set in motion at the Big Bang moment. Perhaps it is notable that the sequence in Genesis 1 mentions the heavens first and the earth second.

According to Albert Einstein's mathematical theory of general relativity, all of space, including earth, was contained in a single point from which the universe has been expanding ever since. The point was something of infinite density containing all of the mass and space-time in the universe before it rapidly expanded in the Big Bang. Because the universe is expanding, it had to have a beginning, and a beginning calls for a creator. The Bible is very clear that God was that creator.

The science-based, old-earth creationist's view is depicted in the figure below and is best understood in the context of the scientific understanding presented starting with the Big Bang at the far left as time zero.

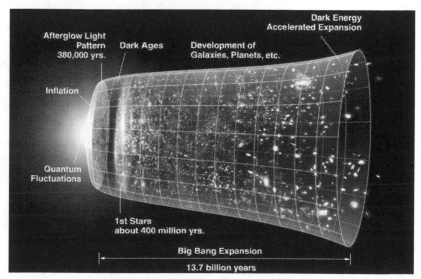

Source: https://en.wikipedia.org/wiki/Big_Bang#/media/File:CMB_Timeline300_no_WMAP.jpg. The image is from NASA and is in the public domain.

It will be noted that there are 14 rings on the cylindrical cone moving from left to right. Each ring represents one billion years, meaning that creation began almost 14 billion years ago. Counting from left to right, earth was created between the 9th and 10th ring. Thus, there is a 9-billion-year span between when the universe creation process began and the creation of the earth. Today we live in the farthest ring to the right, and everything that is spoken of in the Bible happened in that ring. In terms of total time since the creation moment, we are but a speck in time almost 14 billion years away from the initial moment of creation of the universe and about 4.6 billion years away from when earth was created.

What Is Cosmic Time?

Cosmic time (CT) began at the moment of creation of the universe. Cosmic time is the time covered by the physical formation and development of the universe since the Big Bang. Effects that can occur in cosmic time, predicted by Einstein's Theory of Relativity, are different than what one can imagine in geological time. In CT, time can change based on the speed of movement of objects and the gravitational force exerted on an object.

What Is Geological Time?

The geological time scale (GTS) comes from isotopic measurements of the chemical elements in layers of rocks and sediment found in the earth. From artifacts found in these different layers geologists, paleontologists, and archeologists have been able to describe the relationships between events that have occurred throughout the history of the earth. In addition geologsts have been able to trace back in time how the earth may have formed. Measurements are done with scientifically accepted indicators such as isotopes and luminescence, and they provide significant evidence for the validity of geological time.

Thus, paleontologists can determine the ages of fossils of animals and plants by examining them in the context of the layers of rock and sediment in which they are found. Each layer of rock represents a measurable geological time frame (see table below). For example, dinosaur fossils are found in the geological layers belonging to the Jurassic Period, which was

145 to 200 million years ago. In recent years, DNA dating techniques have also been used. From them scientists can also determine when different animals lived.

Because of the order provided by the GTS and the Bible it is possible to assign approximate geological times to the Genesis description of events that took place on each of the seven days and compare them, as in the table below. This in itself is testimony to the convergence of science and the Bible.

Geological Time Compared to Genesis Chapter One Time
MYA=Millions of Years Ago from Present

Day	EON	ERA	PERIOD	MYA
6		Cenzoic	Quaternary	0-2.6
			Neogene	2.6-23
			Paleogene	23-66
5	Phanerozoic	Mesozoic	Cretaceous	66-145
			Jurassic	145-201.3
			Triassic	201.3-252.2
		Paleozoic	Permian	252.2-298.9
			Carboniferous	298.9-358.9
			Devonian	358.9-419.2
			Silurian	419.2-443.4
			Ordovician	443.4-485.4
			Cambrian	485.4-541

Day	EON	ERA	PERIOD	MYA
1-4	Proterozoic	Neoproterozoic	Ediacaran	541-635
			Cryogenian	635-850
			Tonian	850-1000
		Mesoproterozoic	Stenian	1000-1200
			Ectasian	1200-1400
			Calymmian	1400-1600
		Paleoproterozoic	Statherian	1600-1800
			Orosiran	1800-2050
			Rhyacian	2050-2300
			Siderian	2300-2500
	Archean	Neoarchean	No Periods	2500-2800
		Mesoarchean		2800-3200
		Paleoarchean		3200-3600
		Eoarchean		3600-4000
1	Hadean	No Eras	No Periods	4000-4600

The writing of Genesis has been attributed to Moses, who had no understanding of modern science. Moses wrote what the Holy Spirit inspired him to write regarding both the order and substance of the Genesis events. When the extensive scientific dating of these early geological events is viewed together with the events of Genesis, we see a parallel agreement between science and the Bible in terms of the order of the events. When the events occurred is a difference between young and old earth creationists.

However, you will recall that the Hebrew word for *day* in Genesis 1, *yom*, can mean a 24-hour day *or* a very long period of time. Thus, the geological time can agree with Genesis when the interpretation of a day is understood as a longer period of time rather than a 24-hour day.

In this view of geological time, the Bible and science have been reconciled without altering the meaning of Scripture. This is consistent with the words of 2 Peter 3:8: "But do not forget this one thing, dear friends: With the Lord a day is like a thousand years, and a thousand years are like a day."

Also, God has described Himself as "I Am" (Exodus 3: 14). This means he existed before time and will exist beyond time indicating that He is not constrained by time. He is an active God, this activity in His creation having been recorded in the nearly 6000 years of Biblical history. It should not be surprising that His activity was also recorded in geological time during the 4.6 billion years since earth's creation.

Was Our Planet Specially Prepared for Humans?

Data from the scientific disciplines of physics, chemistry, biology, astronomy, and mathematics indicates a universe and an earth created in just the right detail, balance, preciseness, and exquisiteness to support life on earth. As mentioned earlier this is known as the Anthropic Principle.[9]

We are on a planet that appears to have been designed perfectly just for our existence, which should not be surprising in light of God's stated pre-creation plan. Consider a few of the known scientific facts that make up the Anthropic Principle:

- Billions of years of dying stars in the universe, called supernovae, have provided the basic chemical elements necessary to create all matter.
- Lethal radiation from these exploding stars does not reach earth because of the depth of space, providing us a safe distance from the radiation.
- Our own solar system within the Milky Way Galaxy has planets that have removed from our solar orbit debris that would have collided with earth.
- The earth's orbit around the sun is circular rather than elliptical; that plus the fact that we are just the right distance from the sun ensures an earth temperature range that is conducive to life.
- Our sun is just the right size and produces just the right amount of energy to support life.

---

[9] For a detailed discussion of the Anthropic Principle, go to www.godandscience. org/apologetics/designss.html. See also www.privilegedplanet.com and the DVD *The Privileged Planet.*

+ The earth is protected from solar wind by a magnetic field produced from a molten iron core generated by the proper amount of internal radioactivity.

+ Earth's gravity is exactly right to maintain a life-supporting atmosphere of just the right balance of gases.

This all speaks to a creation that appears to be designed, not a product of chance. This grand design goes all the way back to the moment of creation. The physical conditions and energy distributed at the moment of the Big Bang allowed the ultimate creation of an environment suitable for life. Calculations made by Oxford professor of mathematics Roger Penrose show that the likelihood of these conditions being met by chance is only one in ten to the power of 123 (10^{123}). That is, one chance out of a billion, billion, billion repeated more than a billion billion times (cited in Schroeder, 193). In other words, it is impossible that these conditions would have been met by chance.

It appears that God in His timing prepared planet Earth for the creation of Adam and Eve at a special moment in Earth's history. This was in accordance with the eternal plan that He had ordained before the creation of the universe. (Ephesians 1:4-6) As noted above, science tells us that the precision of the creation from the astronomical to the biological enables life on earth. Any slight deviation would create conditions on earth where life could not be supported. Isaiah 45:18 speaks to this: "For this is what the LORD says—he who created the heavens, he is God; he who fashioned and made the earth, he founded it; he did not create it to be empty, but formed it to be inhabited—he says: 'I am the LORD, and there is no other.'" God, in creating the universe, did create it so that the earth could be "tailor-made" for man.[10] So once the planet was prepared to be hospitable for humans, what do the Bible and science say about the creation of man?

---

[10] Another excellent resource on just how our planet is made to support human life is *Improbable Planet: How Earth Became Humanity's Home*, by Hugh Ross.

CHAPTER 8

What About the Origin of Man?

"The body is the biological life support system for the soul."
Tom Southard 2015

A survey by the Pew Research Center on Religion and Public Life states that 98% of scientists connected to the American Association for the Advancement of Science (AAAS) say they believe humans evolved over time and only 2% believe humans existed in their present form from the beginning. That means a rejection of Adam as the first human. As mentioned previously, the scientific community in general does not accept any role of the supernatural or intelligent design in the creation process, including the origin of man. Yet current scientific data points to a possible role of an intelligence.

Models can be developed that include the available scientific understanding to present comparisons in order to contrast the different views in a way that the reader can come to his/her own conclusions. Knowledge, appreciation and an understanding of these models would enable Christians to dialogue better with people who otherwise would never consider entering into a Biblical discussion and ultimately an interest in the Christian faith.

This chapter will introduce four interpretations—or models—for the origin of man. In so doing, we will revisit the concept of evolution discussed in Chapter 6 and the young-earth and old-earth views of creation discussed in Chapter 7.

1. What Is the Young-Earth Model of Man's Origin in Genesis?

The young-earth model, is an interpretation of the Genesis creation without consideration of cosmic or geological time. This literal account is acceptable to many Christians the world over. This model is consistent with God's creation plan as set forth in Ephesians 1:4-6—"he chose us in him before the creation of the world"—and launched in Genesis 1:1—"In the beginning God created the heavens and the earth." Millions of believers are comfortable with this supernatural explanation, which states that the universe and the world were created by God between 6,000 and 10,000 years ago, in six 24-hour days, with God resting on the seventh day. Genesis 1 describes what the early earth was like, then reports an orderly but daily creation of light, sun, moon, oceans, land masses, etc., culminating with the creation of the man in God's image—male and female—the crown of God's creation. Each day mentioned in the Genesis creation narrative is 24 hours and is an acceptable interpretation of *yom*, the Hebrew word for day. Proponents of this model believe that the existing fossil record for plants, animals and man came after the time of their creation six to ten thousand years ago, not millions or billions of years ago. Much of their rejection of old-earth claims is based on the belief that scientific methods dating the fossils are not valid. In this interpretation, Adam and then Eve were created in God's own image as the first humans on Day 6 without any evolvement from an earlier man, or man-like creatures. Accordingly, Eve was the mother of all humans.

Adam and Eve lived in the Garden of Eden, which by the Genesis description is somewhere in the lower Mesopotamia region, in present-day Iraq. Adam was put in the Garden to till the ground and told to eat of any tree but the tree of the knowledge of good and evil. God told Adam that if he ate of that tree he would be like God, knowing the difference between good and evil. Adam and Eve disobeyed God and sinned by eating of this tree. Through this disobedience both physical *and* spiritual death entered the world.

Concerning the migration of humans around the world, this model says that the migration was just as the Bible says, out of the Garden of Eden.

2. What is the Old-Earth Model of Man's Origin in Genesis?

The old-earth interpretation of the creation of man is predicated not on 24-hour days but rather on scientifically-based cosmic time for the universe (13.8 billion years) and geological time for the earth (4.6 billion years). This account is acceptable to many Christians. It is consistent with God's creation plan of choosing us "in him before the creation of the world" (Ephesians 1: 4-6) and of creating the heavens and the earth "in the beginning"(Genesis 1:1) Like Model 1, it goes on to describe the early earth, the orderly creation of light, sun, moon, oceans, land masses, etc., and the creation of the man in God's image and likeness.

The main difference between Model 2 and Model 1 is the interpretation of the Hebrew word for day, *yom*. Here *yom* is interpreted as being a period of time (no limit) rather than 24 hours. This too is a correct interpretation based on Hebrew. The man God created was Adam, and he was created in God's image as the first human (*Homo sapiens*) *without evolvement* from an earlier man. For this reason, many Christians can accept this model.

Another difference between the models is the allowance for the existence of pre-Adamic creatures. In Genesis, Adam was the first of the human species, and no other human was present on the earth at the time of his creation on Day 6. However, the old-earth creation model recognizes that there were pre-Adamic creatures with human-like features. They were called hominids, which were created by God but were considered to have been extinct before Adam and Eve were created. Hominids had human-like features but were considered animals, and dozens of their fossil remains have been discovered and dated, supporting creation over a long period of time. Adam and Eve were created by God as the first male and female of the human species, and as Eve the mother of all future humans. Adam and Eve lived in the same Garden of Eden about the same time frame as in Model 1

Also differing from Model 1, this model dates the creation of Adam based on the genealogy given in Genesis, but it recognizes that only the significant ancestry was listed. Assuming there was additional ancestry lengthens the time at which Adam could have been created back to 40,000 years ago.[11] Concerning the migration of humans around the world, this model states that it began somewhere in or near the Middle East as in the young earth model.

3. What is the Evolution Model?

The theory of evolution, the basis for this Model 3, came about as a result of Charles Darwin's *On the Origin of Species*, published in 1859. It became the foundation for evolutionary biology. The interpretation of the significance of scientific discoveries in paleontology, geology, and biology has been influenced by the thesis of evolutionary biology through natural selection. Although some in the scientific community have raised concerns about the validity of this model, this is the model of man's origin that would be acceptable to the scientists identified in the Pew Research cited above, as well as by all atheists.

The evolution model is a strictly scientific, old-earth explanation that employs cosmic time for the universe and geological time for the earth. This model states that man evolved from an earlier ape-like life form through successive generations of hominids and humans until there was a modern-day human. This model is unacceptable to most Christians because it allows no room for a supernatural creator such as God. Model 3 is based purely on natural selection processes as interpreted from the fossil record; it has gained some additional support from DNA evidence.

While the concept of life forms developing from other life forms had been expressed by philosophers and scientists for centuries, it was Darwin's book that placed evolution front and center. It made sense in light of the emerging fossil record and the classification of living organisms dating from 1735. This was the year that the Swedish scientist Carolus Linnaeus published *Systema Naturae*, grouping all known organisms according to their similarities.

---

[11] The old-earth model used here was developed by Reasons to Believe and based on scientific findings presented in peer-reviewed scientific journals. In addition, it is testable by scientific inquiry. For this model, the reader is encouraged to consult an excellent treatise incorporating biblical truth and applying scientific understanding on the origin of Adam: *Who Was Adam?: A Creation Model Approach to the Origin of Humanity* by Fazale Rana and Hugh Ross.

A common question is, "Are humans related to apes?" Evolutionary theory says, "not apes but the chimpanzee." What follows is an explanation of how evolution arrives at this conclusion using genetic DNA.

Every cell in every species that ever lived contains DNA. Its molecular chains contain four nucleotides whose sequences constitute a genetic code to synthesize a protein. The nucleotide sequence of DNA contains all of the information required to make the protein required for life. These information sequences are called genes. Without genes there is no life.

Sometimes the molecular chains are altered by chemical or physical means resulting in changes that affect the information which DNA passes on. This change is called a mutation. Mutations can be harmful or harmless. Harmful mutations are usually lethal over just a few generations and can result in the disappearance of a living group. Examples of this may have been dinosaurs and the various *Homo* species that lived before the modern *Homo sapiens*. Harmless mutations can pass from generation to generation, affecting change with each subsequent generation. By comparing the DNA of human fossil remains to those of modern-day humans, a picture of how they may have evolved can be created. Without mutation, evolution would not be possible.

The DNA of modern humans, the Homo sapien, is similar to that of the higher primates and other now extinct *Homo* species. Slight differences in the DNA result in the morphological differences between the species. The greater the difference in the DNA, the greater is the species difference. For example, between modern humans existing today all over the world, the DNA is 99.1% the same. Stated another way, today's humans are only 0.9 % different from each other. Every human carries about 3 billion base pairs of nucleotides organized among 22 paired chromosomes. While seemingly small, this 0.9 % difference in DNA leads to 27 million different base pairs, and that gives us our differences in eye color, height, skin color, disease susceptibility, etc. Thus, we are all uniquely different from each other because of this 0.9%. Compared to Neanderthals who lived and went extinct 30,000 years ago, we are 0.5% different. Compared to chimpanzees, we are 1.2% different in DNA, and with gorillas 2% different. These differences are calculated on only the genes that are shared with the modern human.

However, when the entire genome is compared, the differences are much larger. Under this comparison, the chimpanzee to modern human difference is another 4-5%. While we are not related to today's chimpanzee, DNA evidence suggests that today's humans share with today's chimpanzees a common ancestor that lived 6 to 8 million years ago, but today's humans did not evolve along the same branch as any chimpanzees living today. Today's apes developed along a different path from a common ancestor shared by monkeys and apes that lived about 25 million years ago. The evolution view that modern humans had a common ancestor with today's chimpanzee is one reason many Christians reject this position.

Concerning the migration of humans around the world, there have been two explanations of how this was accomplished. One explanation, known as the Multi-Regional Evolution model (MRE), states that different hominids first migrated out of Africa, scattered around the world, and then simultaneously evolved into humans of different races. Hominids, in the evolution model, included early transitional species leading to today's humans.

More recently the MRE has given way to the out-of-Africa model. Generally accepted today, this model advocates the migration out of Africa by humans who had evolved from a single *Homo sapiens* species. As these Homo sapiens migrated around the world, they replaced earlier *Homo* species present in areas that had resulted from earlier migrations.

As a model for the origin of man, evolution is non-theistic, relying 100% on scientific data that it claims supports natural selection. This model does not recognize a pre-creation purpose. Evolution has no position on sin and death would be considered only as a natural end to living.

4. What Is the Theistic Evolution Model?

A fourth model is called theistic evolution (TE). It is an attempt at harmonization of belief in God with scientific findings. In it God uses evolution and natural selection as a creative process to create mankind, culminating in the creation of Adam. It also leaves room for different theistic interpretations.

Theistic evolution holds that the biblical teachings about God and his creation are compatible with contemporary scientific understanding about biological evolution because God used the evolutionary process to create man. TE is not a scientific theory like evolution, but rather a range of views about how the science of general evolution relates to creation views interpreted from the Bible. Theistic evolution states that God used the evolutionary process to create man.

One TE view is that God directed evolution at each and every step, including every mutation. A second view is that God began an initial creation and just let the evolutionary process run without any control. This view would not be in keeping with a creator God who, as described in Ephesians 1:4-6, predestined His creation with a specific person in mind. God directing every step or intervening as necessary would be consistent with predestination.

A third view is that God set the evolutionary process in motion and then intervened at special times to create the kinds of animals he wanted in the sequence he wanted. He entered into the evolutionary process at critical times consistent with scientific explanations of speciation.

Theistic evolution has its critics among orthodox believers. By definition evolution does not acknowledge Adam as the first man, and with some adherents regards the creation account in Genesis, including the Fall of Man through disobedience to God, as a myth. TE believes in old-earth creation over millions of years, during which many animals and early humans died before Adam came on the scene. Rather than seeing Adam's sin as introducing death into the world, TE would say that there was death among all living things before the Fall of Man in the Garden. Sin by Adam in the garden was spiritual death.

This chart summarizes the main points of each of the four models we have discussed, especially as they compare with the Genesis account of creation and the origin of man.

Origin of Man Model Comparisons

Model	Universe Creation	Earth Creation	Plants Created	Human Creation	Physical Death Source	Spiritual Death Source	Did Adam Exist?	God Controlled Creation
1 Young-Earth	Day 1 Gen.1:1	Day 1 Gen.1:1	Day 3 Gen. 1:11	Day 6 Gen. 1:26	Sin	From Adam's Sin	Yes	Yes
2 Old-Earth	13.8 Billion Years Ago (BYA)	4-5 BYA	Over Time	Adam & Eve First	Sin	From Adam's Sin	Yes	Yes

Model	Universe Creation	Earth Creation	Plants Created	Human Creation	Physical Death Source	Spiritual Death Source	Did Adam Exist?	God Controlled Creation
3 Evolution	13.8 BYA	4-5 BYA	Over Time	Evolved	From Living	N/A	No Adam	No
4 Theistic Evolution	13.8 BYA	4-5 BYA	Over Time	Evolved	From Living	Usually From Adam's Sin	Yes	Yes and No

These models present a useful overview of where the Bible and science stand on the creation and origin of man. Knowing them will enable you to engage on an intellectual basis with someone having doubts about the faith or with a spiritual seeker conflicted by the perceived Bible-science conflict.

Model 1 has appeal among many Christians, but there will be disagreement relative to Models 1 and 2, the main differences being young-earth versus old-earth dating and the literal interpretation of Genesis. Believers must exclude Model 3, since it recognizes neither God nor Christ. Models 2 and 4 would be more appealing to the un-churched, particularly those who have a difficult time accepting the six-day creation. Model 4, however, theistic evolution, would face the same Christian objections to evolution mentioned above depending on how one views God's involvement.

I believe that this leaves Model 2 as the most acceptable interpretation of Genesis to present to disengaged Christians and non-believers, for whom the six-day account of creation is an obstacle and need an intellectual explanation that incorporates known science and biblical truth.

One final question remains: Why did God make Adam and Eve? The answer lies in His pre-creation plan revealed in Ephesians 1:4-6 and His intent for the church in Ephesians 3:7-12. No matter which creation model you settle on, do not let your preference for it interfere without first understanding God's plan. This was a plan conceived by God that allowed man to become holy and blameless in His sight through Jesus Christ. It also provided for the Christian church to make known His manifold wisdom to the principalities and powers in heavenly places. Adam and Eve were the initial humans in God's long line of faithful servants who would accomplish God's intent. As a Christian you are part of the church and you are charged to make His manifold wisdom known.

CONCLUSION

"Be on your guard; **stand firm in the faith**; be men of courage; be strong." (1 Corinthians 16:13)

You have completed a study of evidences for a wide range of important theological questions that you have likely raised in your own mind. These questions also represent issues that you will encounter as you go through life. It is important to keep this book as a reference and consult it frequently to keep yourself sharp. People intent on attacking your faith will choose various strategies to do so, and you must be ready to respond confidently.

One basic strategy is to challenge your faith in the existence of God and the reliability of the Bible. This is where you can have the advantage if you know your faith and the evidence. Recalling the apologetics lessons from Part I, always ask anyone challenging your faith to provide evidence for their statements. If they cannot then you know that the statements are not factually based. On the other hand if you have retained the elements of this book you should be able to provide evidence for your beliefs. The most important thing I hope you have learned from this book is that there is historical and scientific evidence supporting the Bible and the truth of the Christian faith. That evidence is there for you to use. God wants you to use it.

Skeptics will also try to create doubts by suggesting that God—if He exists at all—must be neither loving nor omnipotent, given the plagues of disease, birth defects, and death that we all face. Your response is that God causes none of these ills. They have been present since creation, but we will be judged on how we handle them.

Another strategy will be to marginalize and insult you intellectually, especially as skeptics claim that modern science has disproven the Bible. Part II has introduced you to key scientific questions and demonstrated how science actually reinforces biblical claims about the creation of the universe and the origin of man. Keep in mind the convergence of science and theology discussed here as you intellectually present and defend your faith.

Above all make sure you do so with a sound knowledge of the Bible. Be a Bible reader!

Remember, intellectual knowledge and biblical knowledge go hand in hand. They complement each other. If you know the biblical view and the intellectual argument, you will be equipped and ready for any encounter directed at shaking your faith. When you add that to what you learn in a secular classroom on any subject, you automatically have the advantage because you are the most knowledgeable person in the room.

This is because those who attack your faith will generally do so with a lack of biblical knowledge and understanding. They only know their subject, and any attempt they make to dissuade you is based not on fact but only on their opinion. You know the facts, and I hope that you are so trained and equipped that, like the soldier and first responder, your knowledge of the faith will automatically kick in when needed.

What you have learned from this book is college level material, but you are unlikely to hear it in college the way we have presented it here. This is because our premise of God's sovereign involvement—for example, in the creation of the world, the origin of man, and the development of America and Western Civilization—is usually unacceptable in academia. Academics who are hostile to Christianity do not want you to conclude that a causal agent—an intelligence—might be involved, because that could lead you to acknowledge the agent as God.

I urge you to continue reading about the issues raised in this book. Compare what you read to what the Bible says, and be encouraged by 1 Peter 3:15—"Always be prepared to give an answer to everyone who asks you to give the reason for the hope that you have."

You represent the future of the faith and of our country, and they both need you to stand in the gap for God's truth. This will be needed more than at any time in the past. The sovereign God who created the heavens and the earth predestined you to be where you are right now and He desires that you be a soldier for Him and be in relationship with Him forever. That is why He sent Jesus to die for your sins. Don't let him down.

Have a blessed life in service to God; that is what He put you here for.

116

APPENDIX

A. Prophecies About Jesus

	Prophecies About Jesus	Old Testament Scripture	New Testament Fulfillment
1	Messiah would be born of a woman.	Genesis 3:15	Matthew 1:20 Galatians 4:4
2	Messiah would be born in Bethlehem.	Micah 5:2	Matthew 2:1 Luke 2:4-6
3	Messiah would be born of a virgin.	Isaiah 7:14	Matthew 1:22-23 Luke 1:26-31
4	Messiah would come from the line of Abraham.	Genesis 12:3 Genesis 22:18	Matthew 1:1 Romans 9:5
5	Messiah would be a descendant of Isaac.	Genesis 17:19 Genesis 21:12	Luke 3:34
6	Messiah would be a descendant of Jacob.	Numbers 24:17	Matthew 1:2
7	Messiah would come from the tribe of Judah.	Genesis 49:10	Luke 3:33 Hebrews 7:14
8	Messiah would be heir to King David's throne.	2 Samuel 7:12-13 Isaiah 9:7	Luke 1:32-33 Romans 1:3
9	Messiah's throne will be anointed and eternal.	Psalm 45:6-7 Daniel 2:44	Luke 1:33 Hebrews 1:8-12
10	Messiah would be called Immanuel.	Isaiah 7:14	Matthew 1:23
11	Messiah would spend a season in Egypt.	Hosea 11:1	Matthew 2:14-15

	Prophecies About Jesus	Old Testament Scripture	New Testament Fulfillment
12	A massacre of children would happen at Messiah's birthplace.	Jeremiah 31:15	Matthew 2:16-18
13	A messenger would prepare the way for Messiah	Isaiah 40:3-5	Luke 3:3-6
14	Messiah would be rejected by his own people.	Psalm 69:8 Isaiah 53:3	John 1:11 John 7:5
15	Messiah would be a prophet.	Deuteronomy 18:15	Acts 3:20-22
16	Messiah would be preceded by Elijah.	Malachi 4:5-6	Matthew 11:13-14
17	Messiah would be declared the Son of God.	Psalm 2:7	Matthew 3:16-17
18	Messiah would be called a Nazarene.	Isaiah 11:1	Matthew 2:23
19	Messiah would bring light to Galilee.	Isaiah 9:1-2	Matthew 4:13-16
20	Messiah would speak in parables.	Psalm 78:2-4 Isaiah 6:9-10	Matthew 13:10-15; 34-35
21	Messiah would be sent to heal the brokenhearted.	Isaiah 61:1-2	Luke 4:18-19
22	Messiah would be a priest after the order of Melchizedek.	Psalm 110:4	Hebrews 5:5-6
23	Messiah would be called King.	Psalm 2:6 Zechariah 9:9	Matthew 27:37 Mark 11:7-11
24	Messiah would be praised by little children.	Psalm 8:2	Matthew 21:16
25	Messiah would be betrayed.	Psalm 41:9 Zechariah 11:12-13	Luke 22:47-48 Matthew 26:14-16
26	Messiah's price money would be used to buy a potter's field.	Zechariah 11:12-13	Matthew 27: 9-10

	Prophecies About Jesus	Old Testament Scripture	New Testament Fulfillment
27	Messiah would be falsely accused.	Psalm 35:11	Mark 14:57-58
28	Messiah would be silent before his accusers.	Isaiah 53:7	Mark 15:4-5
29	Messiah would be spat upon and struck.	Isaiah 50:6	Matthew 26:67
30	Messiah would be hated without cause.	Psalm 35:19 Psalm 69:4	John 15:24-25
31	Messiah would be crucified with criminals.	Isaiah 53:12	Matthew 27:38 Mark 15:27-28
32	Messiah would be given vinegar to drink.	Psalm 69:21	Matthew 27:34 John 19:28-30
33	Messiah's hands and feet would be pierced.	Psalm 22:16 Zechariah 12:10	John 20:25-27
34	Messiah would be mocked and ridiculed.	Psalm 22:7-8	Luke 23:35
35	Soldiers would gamble for Messiah's garments.	Psalm 22:18	Luke 23:34 Matthew 27:35-36
36	Messiah's bones would not be broken.	Exodus 12:46 Psalm 34:20	John 19:33-36
37	Messiah would be forsaken by God.	Psalm 22:1	Matthew 27:46
38	Messiah would pray for his enemies.	Psalm 109:4	Luke 23:34
39	Soldiers would pierce Messiah's side.	Zechariah 12:10	John 19:34
40	Messiah would be buried with the rich.	Isaiah 53:9	Matthew 27:57-60
41	Messiah would resurrect from the dead.	Psalm 16:10 Psalm 49:15	Matthew 28:2-7 Acts 2:22-32
42	Messiah would ascend to heaven.	Psalm 24:7-10	Mark 16:19 Luke 24:51

	Prophecies About Jesus	Old Testament Scripture	New Testament Fulfillment
43	Messiah would be seated at God's right hand.	Psalm 68:18 Psalm 110:1	Mark 16:19 Matthew 22:44
44	Messiah would be a sacrifice for sin.	Isaiah 53:5-12	Romans 5:6-8

Source: Fairchild, Mary, *Prophesies of Jesus Fullfilled*. Christianity.about.com., April 8, 2016.

B. Recommended Resources

This book is at its core a book of Apologetics something I hope you pursue. As a basis for apologetics it would be worthwhile for you to be aware what may be the bible on apologetics. It is Norman Geisler's *The Big Book of Christian Apologetics, An A to Z Guide* (Baker: Grand Rapids, 2012).

For To Know With Certainty I found these resources—print, online, and video—particularly helpful and commend them to you for further study. They are organized by chapter to help you decide which materials to select. LS

Introduction

Bock, Darrell and Daniel B. Wallace. Video: "The Battle to Dethrone Jesus." The John Ankerberg Show, Program 3, 2007.

Housman, Brian. "Why Are Teens Leaving the Faith?" *Parenting Magazine*, June 17, 2013.

Kinnaman, David and Gabe Lyons. *UnChristian: What a New Generation Really Thinks About Christianity and Why it Matters*. Grand Rapids: Baker Books, 2007.

Kinnaman, David and Aly Hawkins. *You Lost Me: Why Young Christians Are Leaving Church … and Rethinking Faith*. Ada, MI: Baker Books, 2016.

West, John G. "Are Young People Losing Their Faith Because of Science?" Pew Forum on Religion and Public Life, April 2009, www.pewforum. org/files/2009/04/fullreport.pdf.

Chapter 1 - Some Basic Questions

Does God Exist? Five 30-minute video plus lessons and discussion guide. TruU.org.

Hanegraaff, Hank. *Has God Spoken? Proof of the Bible's Divine Inspiration*. Nashville: Thomas Nelson, 2011.

Chapter 2 – Is The New Testament True?

Bierle, Don. *Surprised by Faith.* Third Edition, Faith Search International, 2012.

Habermas, Gary R. and Michael R. Licona. *The Case for the Resurrection of Jesus.* Grand Rapids: Kregel Publications, 2004.

Is The Bible Reliable? - Five 30-minute videos plus lessons and discussion guide. TruU.org.

Metzger, Bruce M. *History of New Testament Textual Criticism.* Grand Rapids: Eerdmans, 1963.

Strobel, Lee. *The Case for Christ: A Journalist's Personal Investigation of the Evidence for Jesus.* Grand Rapids: Zondervan, 1998. (Also as DVD).

Witherington, Ben III. "Why the 'Lost Gospels' Lost Out." *Christianity Today*, June 1, 2004.

Chapter 3 – How Did the Christian Church Develop?

Jones, Timothy Paul. *Christian History Made Easy.* Torrance, CA: Rose Publishing, 2009.

Chapter 4 – What is Your Spiritual DNA?

Barton, David. *America's Godly Heritage.* DVD, 1.5 hours, Aledo, TX.

D'Souza, Dinesh. *What's So Great About Christianity?* Carol Stream, IL: Tyndale House Publishers, 2007.

Chapter 5 – What is Science?

"Intelligent Design versus Naturalism: What about Truth?" 10-minute video, https://www.youtube.com/watch?v=Jm3TDkRWjJohttps://www.youtube.com/watch?v=Jm3TDkRWjJo.

Meyer, Stephen E. *Signature in the Cell: DNA and the Evidence for Intelligent Design.* New York: Harper Collins, 2009.

Schroeder, Gerald L. *The Science of God: The Convergence of Scientific and Biblical Wisdom.* New York: Free Press, 2009.

Chapter 6 – What is Evolution?

Behe, Michael. *Darwin's Black Box: The Biochemical Challenge to Evolution.* New York: The Free Press, 1996.

Rana, Fazale. *Through the Lens: Evolution Under the Microscope.* DVD. http://shop.reasons.org/product-p/d1501.htm.

Revolutionary: Michael Behe and the Mystery of Molecular Machines. 60-minute DVD. Discovery Institute, 2016.

Chapter 7 – What About Creation?

"How Old Is the Universe? Astronomers Debate the Scientific Evidence." Six hours of video. John Ankerberg Show, jashow.org.

Ross, Hugh. *Probability of Life on Earth.* Reasons to Believe, RTB30, April 2, 2004.

Ross, Hugh. *Improbable Planet: How Earth Became Humanity's Home.* Grand Rapids: Baker Books, 2016.

Chapter 8 – What About The Origin of Man?

Rana, Fazale and Hugh Ross. *Who Was Adam? A Creation Model Approach to the Origin of Humanity.* 2nd ed. Covina, CA: RTB Press, 2015.

REFERENCES

Axe, Douglas. *Undeniable: How Biology Confirms Our Intuition That Life is Designed*. New York: Harper One, 2016.

Barna, George. *Third Millennium Teens: Research on the Minds, Hearts and Soul of America's Teenagers*. Barna Research Group, 1999).

Barna Research Group. https://www.barna.com/research/parents-accept-responsibility-for-their-childs-spiritual-development-but-struggle-with-effectiveness/. May 6, 2003.

———. "Six Reasons Young Christians Leave Church." Sept. 28, 2011. https://www.barna.org/teens-next-gen-articles/528-six-reasons-young-christians-leave-church.

Behe, Michael. *Darwin's Black Box: The Biochemical Challenge to Evolution*. New York: The Free Press, 1996.

Berean Study Bible (BSB).

Biblica. *In What Language Was The Bible Written, Biblica*, December 27, 2013. From 55 or so:

Bierle, Don. *Surprised by Faith* Lynwood, MA: Emerald Books, 1992.

Billy Graham Evangelistic Association. "Answers." June 1, 2004.

BioLogos. http://biologos.org/blog/a-survey-of-clergy-and-their-views-on-origins. May 8, 2013.

Blanshard, Paul. "Three Cheers for Our Secular State." *The Humanist*, March/April, 17, 1976, 25.

Bock, Darrell and Daniel B. Wallace. "The Battle to Dethrone Jesus." The John Ankerberg Show, Program 3, 2007.

christianity.about.com/od/biblefactsandlists/a/Prophecies-Jesus.htm

Clement. Epistle 1 Chapter 42.

Cross, F.L. *The Oxford Dictionary of the Christian Church*, 3rd rev. ed. Oxford: Oxford University Press, 2005.

D'Souza, Dinesh. *What's So Great About Christianity?* Tyndale House Publishers, 2007.

Darwin, Charles. *On the Origin of Species by Means of Natural Selection, Or the Preservation of Favoured Races in the Struggle for Life.* 6th Ed. London: John Murray, 1876.

DarwinThenAndNow.com.

Dawkins, Richard. *The God Delusion.* Boston: Houghton Mifflin Harcourt, 2006.

———. *The Greatest Show on Earth: The Evidence for Evolution.* UK: Free Press, 2009.

DissentFromDarwin.org.

Ecklund, Elaine Howard. "Religion and Spirituality among University Scientists," Feb. 5, 2007, http://religion.ssrc.org/reforum/Ecklund.pdf.

Ecklund, E. H. and C. P. Scheitle. "Religion among Academic Scientists: Distinctions, Disciplines, and Demographics." *Social Problems* 54:2007, 289–307.

Ehrman, Bart D. *From Jesus to Constantine: A History of Early Christianity.* Chantilly, VA: The Great Courses.

———. *Jesus, Interrupted: Revealing the Hidden Contradictions in the Bible (And Why We Don't Know About Them).* New York: Harper Collins, 2009.

Farlex, Inc. *TheFreeDictionary.com.*

Fitzmyer, Joseph A. "The Language of Palestine in the First Century A.D." *The Catholic Biblical Quarterly* 32 (1970): 501-531.

Funker, Cary and Becky Alper. "Highly religious Americans are less likely than others to see conflict between faith and science." Pew Research Center, Oct. 22, 2015.

Gallup Poll. Jan-Nov 2011.

Graffin, Gregory W. and William B. Provine. "Evolution, Religion and Free Will." *American Scientist* 95 (July-August 2007): 294-297. (Cf. also www.polypterus.com/results.pdf).

Gross, Neil and Solon Simmons. "How Religious are America's College and University Professors?" Social Science Research Council, February 6, 2007, http://religion.ssrc.org/reforum/Gross_Simmons.pdf, p. 5.

———. "The Religiosity of American College and University Professors." *Sociology of Religion* 70 (2009): 101-129.

Habermas, Gary R. and Michael R. Licona. *The Case for the Resurrection of Jesus*. Grand Rapids: Kregel Publications, 2004.

Hallquist, Chris. *Why atheists don't think the Bible is historically reliable*. Patheos, The Incredible HallQ, http://www.patheos.com/blogs/hallq/2012/07/why-atheists-dont-think-the-bibl-is-historically-reliable/,July 2012).

Hanegraaff, Hank. *Has God Spoken? Proof of the Bible's Divine Inspiration*. Nashville: Thomas Nelson, 2011.

Harris, Stephen L. *Understanding the Bible*: Palo Alto: Mayfield, 1985.

GotQuestions.org. http://www.gotquestions.org/heavenly-places-realms.html#ixzz3DQAfuJjZ

Hengel, Martin.

Housman, Brian. *Why Are Teens Leaving the Faith? Parenting Magazine*, June 17, 2013.

Irenaeus. *Against Heresies* I:10:1

Jeffrey, Grant R. *The Signature of God*, 3rd ed. Colorado Springs: WaterBrook & Multnomah, 2010.

Jones, Timothy Paul. *Christian History Made Easy*. Torrance, CA: Rose Publishing, 2009.

Josephus, Flavius. *Antiquities of the Jews*, Book 18, Chapter 3, 3.

Kennedy, D. James. *What if Jesus Had Never Been Born: The Positive Impact of Christianity in History*. Nashville: Thomas Nelson, 1982.

Kinnaman, David and Gabe Lyons. *Good Faith*. Grand Rapids: Baker Books, 2016.

Kinnaman, David and Aly Hawkins. *You Lost Me: Why Young Christians Are Leaving Church ... and Rethinking Faith*. Ada, MI: Baker Books, 2016.

Krauss, Lawrence. "A response and perspective on debate with Craig." Facebook, April 4, 2011 at 11:22pm.

LifeWay Research. http://www.lifeway.com/Article/Research-Poll-Pastors-oppose-evolution-split-on-earths-age. 1/9/2012.

———. "Protestant Pastors' Views on Creation: Survey of 1,000 Protestant Pastors," 1/9/2012.

———. https://cjts3rs.wordpress.com/2012/01/21/lifeway-poll-pastors-oppose-evolution-split-on-earths-age/.

Lincoln, Abraham. "The Perpetuation of Our Political Institutions: Address Before the Young Men's Lyceum of Springfield, Illinois," January 27, 1838.

Lovell, Graham. http://newtestamenthistory.blogspot.com/2012/05/papias-on-mark-and-matthew.html.

Martin, Robert. https://atheistforum.wordpress.com/2014/04/04/did-jesus-really-rise-from-the-dead/.

Masci, David. "On Darwin Day, 5 facts about the evolution debate." Pew Research Center, FacTank, News in the Numbers. Feb. 12, 2016.)

McConnell, Scott. http://www.LifeWay.com/Article/LifeWay-Research-finds-reasons-18-to-22-year-olds-drop-out-of-church. August 7, 2007.

McGee, Matthew. "Chronology of Apostle Paul's Journeys and Epistles." www.matthewmcgee.org. 1998.

Metzger, Bruce M. *History of New Testament Textual Criticism.* Grand Rapids: Eerdmans, 1963.

Meyer, Stephen E. *Signature in the Cell: DNA and the Evidence for Intelligent Design.* New York: Harper Collins, 2009.

Miller, Stanley L. "Production of Amino Acids under Possible Primitive Earth Conditions" *Science.* **117** (3046): 528–9 (1953).

——— and Harold C. Urey. "Organic Compound Synthesis on the Primitive Earth." *Science.* 130 No. 3370 (1959): 245–51.

New Living Translation (NLT).

Oxford English Dictionary Online. https://en.oxforddictionaries.com.

Penrose, Roger. *The Emperor's New Mind: Concerning Computers, Minds and the Laws of Physics.* New York: Penquin Books, 1991.

Pew Research Center. "America's Changing Religious Landscape." May 12, 2015.

———. "Public Praises Science; Scientists Fault Public, Media." July 9, 2009.

Pinsent, Andrew. "What The Church Has Given the World." *Catholic Herald,* May 6, 2011.

Plantinga, Alvin. *Journal of Science and Theology.*

———. *Knowledge and Christian Belief.* Grand Rapids, MI, Cambridge, UK: William B. Eerdmans, 2015.

Potter, Charles F. *Humanism: A New Religion.* New York: Simon and Schuster, 1930.

Powell, Kara E. and Chap Clark. *Sticky Faith: Everyday Ideas to Build Lasting Faith in Your Kids*. Grand Rapids: Zondervan, 2011.

Rana, Fazale. *Through the Lens: Evolution Under the Microscope*. DVD http://shop.reasons.org/product-p/d1501.htm

——— and Hugh Ross. *Origins of Life: Biblical and Evolutionary Models Face Off.*

Colorado Springs: Navpress, 2004.

——— and Hugh Ross. *Who Was Adam? A Creation Model Approach to the Origin of Humanity*. 2nd Ed. Covina, CA: RTB Press, 2015.

Reece, Jane B. et al. *Campbell Biology*, 9th ed. San Francisco: Benjamin Cummings Publishing Co., 2010.

Riboulet, L. *Histoire de la pédagogie*. Paris, 1925.

Ross, Hugh. *The Genesis Question: Scientific Advances and the Accuracy of Genesis*, 2nd ed. Colorado Springs: Navpress, 2001

Ross, Hugh. *Probability of Life on Earth*. Reasons to Believe, RTB30, April 2, 2004.

———. *Improbable Planet: How Earth Became Humanity's Home*. Grand Rapids, MI: Baker Books, 2016.

Schmidt, Alvin J. *How Christianity Changed the World*. Grand Rapids, MI: Zondervan, 2004.

Schroeder, Gerald L. *The Hidden Face of God: Science Reveals the Ultimate Truth*. New York: Free Press, 2002.

———. *The Science of God: The Convergence of Scientific and Biblical Wisdom*. New York: Free Press, 2009.

Smith, Christian and Robert Faris. *Religion and American Adolescent Delinquency, Risk Behaviors and Constructive Social Activities*. National Study of Youth and Religion, 2002. www.youthandreligion.org.

Stansberry, Cheryl L. "The Influence of Christianity on Western Civilization." *Journal of Cross and Quill*. 2007. http://crossandquill.com/journey/the-influence-of-christianity-on-western-civilization/ May 8, 2013.

Stark, Rodney. *For the Glory of God: How Monotheism Led to Reformations, Science, Witch-Hunts, and the End of Slavery*. Princeton: Princeton University Press, 2003.

Stewart, John. *The Evolutionary Manifesto: Our Role in the Future Evolution of Life*. http://www.evolutionarymanifesto.com.

Strobel, Lee. *The Case for Christ: A Journalist's Personal Investigation of the Evidence for Jesus*. Grand Rapids: Zondervan, 1998. (Also as DVD).

stronginfaith.org/article.php?page=9.

Tacitus. *Annals* 15.44.

"The Bridge Illustration—simple enough to do on a napkin." http://www.extendgrace.org/PDF/spiritual%20conversation%20tools.pdf

Theobald, Douglas L. "29+ Evidences for Macroevolution: The Scientific Case for Common Descent." *The Talk.Origins Archive*. Vers. 2.89. 2012. Web. 12 Mar. 2012 http://www.talkorigins.org/faqs/comdesc/)

Thrombocyte.com. "10-Step Process of Blood Coagulation." 2016.

West, John G. "Are Young People Losing Their Faith Because of Science?" Pew Forum on Religion and Public Life, April 2009, http://www.pewforum.org/files/2009/04/fullreport.pdf.

Willmann, Otto. *The Science of Education in Its Sociological and Historical Aspects*, Vol. I. Beatty, PA: Archabbey Press, 1922.

Witherington, Ben III. "Why the 'Lost Gospels' Lost Out." *Christianity Today*, June 1, 2004.

Woods, Thomas E. Jr. "History Shows Contributions of Catholic Church to Western Civilization." Fredericksburg, VA: *The Free Lance-Star*, December 28, 2001.

———. "The Catholic Church and the Creation of the University." *LewRockwell.com*, May 16, 2005.

Yancey, Philip. "Faith and Doubt." http://philipyancey.com/q-and-a-topics/faith-and-doubt

Yarbrough, Mark. "The Plague of Biblical Illiteracy." *Decision Magazine*, May, 2015.

Printed in the United States
By Bookmasters